the pocket rhubarb cookbook

Nina Mukerjee Furstenau

For the grandmothers, Cecelia Furstenau and Mary Sanning

Printed in the United States of America

First edition 2025

ISBN: 9781953368980

Belt Publishing

6101 Penn Avenue

Suite 201

Pittsburgh PA 15206

www.beltpublishing.com

Cover art by David Wilson

Page design by Julie Foster

contents

Quick Breads, Muffins, Scones, Pancakes + Cakes

Cookies

Mains

Refreshing Drinks

Jams, Chutneys + Preserves

Syrups, Sauces + Relishes

Kitchen Tips

Introduction

The bounty growing in our soil is the ultimate story of humankind. Three times a day, my own body tells me I'm on to something. Working as a food journalist confirms it. But my journey with rhubarb began before this realization about food stories, about the plants we eat, about the soil. It started well before the first reddish-green stalk hit my kitchen counter.

Rhubarb is not something my family spent a lot of time considering before settling in Kansas. We come from northeast India, from stock more interested in lime and eggplant and cilantro. However, in the spring, rhubarb pies would show up with regularity at 4-H gatherings and school suppers in Pittsburg, Kansas. I was intrigued. A sour pie? The only sour notes my palate was used to were bottled up in my mother's lime pickles, which I had no desire at the time to nibble on. But I sure did try those lovely desserts with their mix of tartness and sweet comfort. Later, when I married a Missouri farm boy, rhubarb became a pie of legend. Long-deceased grandmothers from both sides of his American-German-Swedish family had made it from cuttings off plants growing along their back fences, and it lived long in memory. The back garden rhubarb trail also connected to my plate when Missouri small-town church picnics featured it on their expansive tables of tasty goodies. Along with gooseberries and sour cherries, rhubarb made me a forever fan of sour pies and spring.

Plus, you can't go wrong with rhubarb for drama in the garden. The leaves are large, heart-shaped, smooth, and have ruffled edges. The stalks, often red, are sturdy. It's a bonanza of handsomeness, especially when you consider rhubarb also makes delightful eating. Technically, rhubarb is a vegetable with stalks similar to celery. Botanically, it's from the same family as sorrel and buckwheat. In the kitchen, it's most often used as a fruit, in pies, of course, but also savory dishes with tart accents.

Due to that particular flavor profile, the custom of eating rhubarb in pies or tarts or crumbles is more or less everywhere in the world. It's eaten in Britain and the United States, Australia and New Zealand, Northern Europe, Canada, and in the Islamic world, where it has been in culinary use since the tenth century. It has a long history of use in ancient Chinese medicine, and in ancient Arab, Greek, and Roman civilizations. A variety, *Gunnera tinctoria*, or Chilean rhubarb, is eaten in South America. Many Germans relish rhubarb in the spring and link its flavor to a tongue-twister song about "Barbara's Rhabarberbar," or Barbara's rhubarb bar. In fact, as soon as the green tips of spring daffodils and jonquils push through the soil, the hyper-compound German words in the lyrics about Barbara, her rhubarb cake, and her customers often resonate in German towns and on social media, along with a surge of humorous guffaws with German accents. In the US, rhubarb was seeded throughout the country by settlers from Germany and other European nations who were already familiar with the plant.

There's something placeless and even alien about this plant that is known throughout the world. Its exact origins are slightly mysterious (though mostly determined to be southeastern China). The vigorous plant came up in my own garden in the Pacific Northwest when I had a spot there to call my own, and I was stunned by its height—well over my head, with its otherworldly-looking red stalks and leaves that seemed to fan the air in broad strokes. In my Missouri home, rhubarb plants are more subtle, growing two to four feet tall, their heart-shaped leaves tickling the air with their frills.

In cooler climates, the rhubarb season can go all summer. In Missouri, it usually lasts only a few weeks. This short season can make rhubarb feel sensational when it emerges. In a mission to find, process (i.e., strip the leaves and chop the stalks into half-inch and one-inch pieces), and freeze enough rhubarb to test the recipes in this book, and keep some just because, I made a haul: forty pounds of rhubarb, sourced from the farmers' market, the Amish grocery, and our local natural foods store. If you do this, be sure to freeze your rhubarb in a single layer on a baking sheet and bag the pieces afterward. It will save you fighting clumps in your freezer bags and a lot of banging against your countertop to free up small portions. Fair warning: forty pounds of rhubarb creates a very large mound of reddish-green chopped pieces. You are much more likely to be handling a smaller amount.

As I worked with the rhubarb, I began to see how this plant ended up across the US and world. First, it's pretty. Second, it adds a lot of zip to everything you make with it. Third, and this is especially for the nutritionists out there, it gives your body a dose of vitamin A, vitamin C, vitamin K, potassium, manganese, magnesium, folate, riboflavin, niacin, iron, and phosphorus. Fourth, and perhaps most importantly, it tastes like spring.

WORLD HISTORY OF RHUBARB

Cooking up remedies—not culinary dishes—preoccupied many in the early years of humanity, and rhubarb was discovered to have immense value as medicine. Researchers such as Clifford M. Foust in *Rhubarb: The Wondrous Drug* say there probably has been no medicine that has brought greater relief to larger numbers of people than has the powder made from the roots of medicinal rhubarb.

What does rhubarb do for health? Everyone—botanists, horticulturists, merchants, explorers, physicians, pharmacists, and grandmothers—considered rhubarb a mild and dependable relief from ailments of digestion, bowels, and constipation. The ancient Greek physician Pedanius Dioscorides described rhubarb and its properties in his *De Materia Medica* (written between 50 and 70 CE), but long before that, rhubarb's medicinal use was part of life in China. In early Chinese oral wisdom, rhubarb was said to be a purgative (or laxative) and was also used to ease symptoms of malaria and delirious speech while feverish. Its most common use, though, was as a general supplement for anyone to regain or preserve good health and a sense of well-being. Later, the preface to the medical reference book *Bencao*

Gangmu, compiled by Li Shizhen in the sixteenth century, quotes legends about the Divine Farmer (who taught people how to cook and thus civilized humanity), connects medicine and food, and mentions rhubarb as a helpful purgative.

Across the continents, rhubarb root with its cathartic/laxative/restorative effects was just what the world needed. To great consternation in the West, it was learned that these fine medicinal plants did not grow in Europe but came from somewhere east of the Volga River, whose early name was thought to be Rha. "Rha" is also found in *rhabarbarum*, the Latin word for rhubarb. Rhubarb, native to the colder climates in highland China, Mongolia, and Siberia, caused a mad scramble, and not surprisingly, great fortunes for traders were made as rhubarb trundled along trade routes westward, becoming increasingly expensive along the way.

Rhubarb remained costly until the early 1800s, not-so-incidentally when the price of sugar came down. In addition, other varieties of rhubarb more suited to European soils and climate, such as the Siberian *R. undulatum*, were developed for culinary uses. But it was humanity's sweet tooth and the establishment of sugar plantations on the larger Caribbean islands that made it possible for rhubarb's culinary uses to flourish, often at the expense of enslaved people and, later, indentured workers. Those grim conditions of labor reduced the cost of sugar enough that many more households could afford to buy it for use in the large amounts needed for cooking rhubarb pies and tarts.

There are many varieties of rhubarb around the world, but the one common in North America today is garden rhubarb (*Rheum rhabarbarum*). It grows in many parts of the world after having emerged from East Asia and prefers cooler environments over excess heat. This is the plant we love for culinary uses and is the star of this book.

RHUBARB HISTORY IN THE UNITED STATES

Ben Franklin is sometimes credited with sending America's first rhubarb seeds to his friend John Bartram (1699–1777), a well-known botanist in Philadelphia, from London in 1770. However, it is suspected Bartram had already been growing rhubarb since the 1730s from seed sent by another friend, the Quaker Peter Collinson. Regardless, rhubarb did not become popular in the US for culinary purposes for nearly one hundred years, when it began to appear in New England markets and seed catalogs around the 1820s.

ABOVE: Illustrated title page of Mrs. Rundell's *A New System of Domestic Cookery* (London, 1810).

OPPOSITE: An early rhubarb recipe by Mrs. Rundell.

Rhubarb Tart.

Cut the stalks in lengths of four or five inches, and take off the thin skin. If you have a hot hearth, lay them in a dish, and put over a thin syrup of sugar and water, cover with another dish, and let it simmer very slowly an hour—or do them in a block-tin saucepan.

When cold, make into a tart, as codlin. When tender, baking the crust will be sufficient.

One early adopter of rhubarb for home cooks was the widow Maria Eliza Rundell (1745–1828), who published *A New System of Domestic Cookery, formed upon principles of economy, and adapted to the uses of private families* in 1806, originally compiled for her daughters. Her book went far beyond family use, becoming a bestseller and going on to sixty-five editions in the first half of the nineteenth century. The recipe for rhubarb tart in the *New Systems of Domestic Cookery* mentions cooking the rhubarb for one hour—today's rhubarb, long cultivated for tenderness, would be jam if cooked that long. Modern recipes might call for five to ten minutes of cooking time.

The Boston editions of Rundell's book helped establish demand for rhubarb in America. Plus, the timing of rhubarb harvest helped its rise in popularity. Often, in Great Britain and the US, stored apples had shriveled or rotted by spring, just when rhubarb was beginning to flourish. Rhubarb soon became enormously popular in baking and was so favored it was and sometimes still is called the "pie plant."

The US also played a role in why we often consider rhubarb a fruit, though it is actually a vegetable. In 1947, the US Customs Court of Buffalo, New York, reasoned that because rhubarb was used like a fruit for culinary purposes, it must be considered legally a fruit for tax purposes.

HOW TO CHOOSE RHUBARB FOR COOKING

By May, rhubarb plants are at their peak and ready to contribute color, tang, and freshness to your meals. The climate in some locations provides rhubarb through much of the summer, but in my part of the world the whole point of rhubarb may just be to celebrate its fleeting season. Rhubarb is a trustworthy signal that spring has arrived.

When selecting and using rhubarb, choose firm stems with a bright, glossy appearance when they are eight to fifteen inches long. Avoid overly thick stalks, as they may be tough with fibrous or hollow insides. Too-thin stems may lack flavor, and it's best to avoid wilted stems, too. Pick stalks with smaller leaves, if possible, as it probably indicates age of the plant, and make sure those rambling leaves, which contain poisonous oxalic acid, are removed before cooking.

If you are lucky enough to have rhubarb growing in your garden, you'll know it's most tender and flavorful in spring and early summer, though it can be used in cooking throughout the season. To harvest, twist off the leafstalk at the soil line and cut off the leaf. According to the University of Wisconsin–Madison, do not harvest more than a third of the stalks in any year to keep the plant going strong (and don't pull any stalks during the first year of growth). On young plants, pick stalks only in the spring and allow them to grow unpicked all summer, or growth will be delayed the following spring. You can harvest sparingly on vigorous, well-established plants throughout the summer. Any stalks remaining at the end of the season can be pulled just before the first fall frost.

HOW TO PREPARE RHUBARB FOR COOKING

Wash the stems, trim any remaining leaf and root areas, cut stems into pieces, and use in your favorite recipes. Tightly wrapped, unwashed stalks of rhubarb will keep in a refrigerator for several days. Or, to freeze rhubarb, cut clean stalks into half-inch slices and place on a cookie sheet in a single layer to freeze. Repeat this as many times as needed to complete the task of freezing your haul of rhubarb. You can then pack in freezer-safe containers or plastic bags and freeze through without stalks sticking together. It will keep in the freezer for up to six months. Using frozen rhubarb in recipes often works very well and is simple—measure it while frozen and use. If it needs to be thawed, measure it when frozen, thaw it in a colander, and do not press the liquid out. Then, follow the usual recipe steps. Many recipes in this book work just as well with frozen or fresh rhubarb.

RHUBARB AND NUTRITION

The nutrient content in rhubarb boasts good quantities of vitamin K, which helps bone health, and fiber. Rhubarb is said to help with inflammation and fight free radicals that cause skin damage, among other benefits. Healthline breaks down the nutritional value of a 3.5-ounce serving as follows:

Calories: 116 with added
  granulated sugar
Carbohydrates: 31.2 grams
Fiber: 2 grams
Protein: 0.4 grams

Vitamin K1: 18% DV
Calcium: 11% DV
Vitamin C: 4% DV
Potassium: 2% DV
Folate: 1% DV

In 2023, studies cited by Healthline showed emodin, resveratrol, and other chemicals in rhubarb may also contribute to its role in regulating lipid metabolism and lowering bad cholesterol levels. And, as the Old World discovered, the fiber in rhubarb helps keep things moving through your digestive tract, preventing problems such as constipation. Rhubarb also contains compounds called sennosides, which act as natural laxatives, and tannins that provide antidiarrheal effects.

Rhubarb is a rich source of antioxidants. One 2012 study cited by Healthline suggests that the total polyphenol content in rhubarb may be even higher than that of kale. Anthocyanins, which are responsible for its red color, are the same ones found in some fruits, red wine, and cocoa, and are thought to provide health benefits. These antioxidants may also be responsible for some of the health benefits seen with fruits, red wine, and cocoa.

PLANTING RHUBARB

Rhubarb is a perennial, so if you'd like a rhubarb plant of your own, choose a permanent location with enough space for mature plants. Prepare the planting site in the fall by eliminating perennial weeds and working in manure, compost, or other organic matter. Incorporate fertilizer just before planting in the spring.

Rhubarb grows easily in areas with cool winters, where plants may live and produce stalks for harvesting for ten to fifteen years. In cool climates, choose a location that receives at least six hours of direct sun each day. Since rhubarb wilts in hot weather, choose a semi-shaded area protected from the afternoon sun in warm, temperate, and sub-tropical climates. Varieties more suited to warmer climates tend to have greener stalks and shorter lifespans, though the flavor for cooking is as tasty.

Rhubarb typically grows two to four feet tall, with large, smooth, heart-shaped basal leaves. The plant grows from large, fleshy, reddish-brown rhizomes with yellow interiors. The leaves emerge from crown buds when temperatures begin to exceed 40°F in early spring. The thick red or green leafstalks (petioles) grow up to eighteen inches long and one to two inches in diameter and have leaf blades up to a foot or more in width. The foliage dies back to the ground each winter.

Most gardeners think of their vegetable garden beds when considering rhubarb. But its leafy drama makes it an edible alternative in an ornamental planting area. The big leaves contrast exceptionally well with more delicate plants such as red penstemon, bearded iris, tall garden phlox, or ornamental grasses, according to horticulture information from the University of Wisconsin–Madison.

Plantings of purchased crown pieces or divisions from other plantings are best about three feet apart. Set the pieces so the buds are about two inches below the soil surface. Don't harvest any stalks the first year; wait until the second or third year so the roots can establish themselves.

VARIETIES

Though the red-stemmed rhubarb varieties are often preferred, there are also green and speckled (pink) types. Red stalks are not necessarily sweeter, but some feel they are "prettier" when cooked. Many times, the same variety has different names in different areas, as the plants get moved around or they are found in backyards or abandoned farmsteads and become known as heirloom varieties.

Some of the most common varieties posted by the University of Wisconsin–Madison Master Gardener website (https://hort.extension.wisc.edu/articles/rhubarb-rheum-rhabarbarum/) are excerpted here:

☐ **CANADA RED** produces shorter, more slender stalks than other varieties but is tender and very sweet with good red color. It tends to produce few seed stalks.

- **CHERRY RED** (also known as **CHERRY** or **EARLY CHERRY**) has long, thick stalks that are a rich red inside and out. This vigorous producer is juicy, tender, and sweet.

- **CRIMSON RED** (also called **CRIMSON**, **CRIMSON CHERRY**, or **CRIMSON WINE**) produces tall, plump, brightly colored red stalks.

- **MACDONALD** produces well and has tender skin on the brilliant red stalks.

- **VALENTINE** has broad, deep red stalks that retain a good rosy color when cooked. It is much less acid than green-stalked and other red varieties and produces few or no seed stalks.

- **VICTORIA** is a speckled type that produces medium-sized stalks with good flavor. Though there is variation in stalk color depending on the strain, generally, the light green stalks develop pink speckling, especially at the bottom of the stalk.

SOIL PREFERENCES

For best growth, if you have heavy clay soil or very wet soils, plant rhubarb in raised beds for good drainage.

Overly wet conditions may rot the crowns (the central growing point made up of a leafless bundle of roots) over the winter. The best soil for rhubarb is well-drained and high in organic matter. Once established, rhubarb needs little ongoing maintenance. Pick a spot in full sun where the plant can remain for the several years of its lifespan undisturbed.

MODERN MEDICINAL AND ENVIRONMENTAL USES OF RHUBARB

In addition to tasty desserts and savory stews, rhubarb is once again being used as medicine. It has joined the growing list of "superfoods" because it is packed with vitamins C and K, is high in fiber, and contains calcium. Rhubarb extract is also being investigated as a chemotherapy agent, as reported on a range of websites such as American Institute for Cancer Research and WebMD, to stop the spread of some cancers and to trigger cell death (apoptosis) in some tumors; as a cholinesterase inhibitor to help treat the symptoms of Alzheimer's disease and other dementia disorders; as an antimicrobial drug; and as an antioxidant. The ancients felt that rhubarb was good for you, and people today increasingly agree.

In the environment, gardeners such as Louise Riotte, author of *Carrots Love Tomatoes* and other books, extoll the biochemical attributes of rhubarb to battle garden pests. She recommends companion-planting of rhubarb with columbines to keep away spider mites. She also describes a spray made by boiling rhubarb leaves that can protect roses from pests and diseases.

The recipes in this book span some of the very best ways to eat rhubarb, from the beloved desserts to barbecue sauces and refreshing drinks (strawberry rhubarb daiquiris, anyone?), plus a host of meat-based and vegetarian mains and, of course, pie. Make the pies—please, make the pies—but I hope this collection also inspires you to look beyond the expected to see all the magic potential of rhubarb.

pies +
cobblers

Rhubarb Custard Pie

I made this pie for my husband's family's Fourth of July gathering in honor of matriarch Grandma Sanning. The family lore says she made rhubarb into not only a custard pie but also as a buckle (recipe on page 42), which I tried to re-create. Taste it for yourself. Rhubarb Custard Pie is excellent for tables anytime using fresh or frozen rhubarb. In my oven, it needed a full fifty minutes at 350°F after the initial fifteen minutes at 425°F. Let me just say, it was worth the wait. If you use an all-butter crust (recipe on page 51), my personal favorite, it will absorb some of the rhubarb juices in a sublime paring. This is a pie for those who appreciate a balance of sweet with sour. It's for those who like flaky crust, creamy custardy filling, and the soothingly cool reward of vanilla ice cream.

Serves 6–8

All-butter pastry for a double-crust pie, unbaked (recipe on
    page 51)
4 cups ½-inch pieces, coarsely sliced, fresh or frozen
    rhubarb (thawed)
1½ cups granulated sugar
¼ cup all-purpose flour
1½ teaspoons grated orange zest

½ teaspoon grated nutmeg

¼ teaspoon cinnamon

¼ teaspoon salt

3 eggs, beaten

2 tablespoons cold butter, cut into 6–8 pieces

Glaze for pastry:

1 egg yolk

1 teaspoon water

Turbinado sugar for sprinkling the top pastry lattice

Preheat the oven to 425°F. For best results, make your pastry a couple of hours ahead of time, wrap two disks in cellophane, and chill in the refrigerator until you are ready to roll out the pie shell. On a lightly floured surface, or on a large section of parchment paper lightly dusted with flour, roll out the larger portion of dough to about 12–13 inches in diameter. Loosely drape it into a 9-inch pie plate without stretching the dough. There should be some overhang. Lightly press the dough to conform to the bottom of the pie plate, pricking it with a fork at intervals along the bottom. Roll out the second round to a 11- to 12-inch round and cut the pastry into strips about ¾ inch wide. Set aside.

In a large bowl, combine the rhubarb, sugar, flour, orange zest, nutmeg, cinnamon, and salt; stir in the eggs to blend, and fold in the butter. Turn the rhubarb filling into the prepared pie shell. Evenly space five strips of pastry over the filling and weave five more through them in the opposite direction to make a lattice top. Press the overhanging strips to the rim and decoratively crimp to seal. To glaze the pie crust, beat the egg yolk in a small bowl with 1 teaspoon of water and paint onto the strips; you will have leftover egg mixture. Sprinkle the lattice strips with turbinado sugar. Bake the pie for 15 minutes, then reduce the oven temperature to 350°F and bake for 45–50 minutes longer until the crust is golden brown and the filling is bubbly. Cool on a rack for 1 hour or more.

Rhubarb Strawberry Pie

This flavor combination has stood the test of time, and I'm here to vouch for it. It has hard-to-resist flavor, and it's also pretty. If you're reading this recipe, I'm fairly sure you're someone who wraps up good feelings in pastry and offers it to your community or family on the regular, or wants to. You'll be joining generations of cooks all over the US who made this for families as soon as the rhubarb stalks growing along the back of the garden got tall enough. Go ahead, follow in their loving footsteps.

Serves 8

1¼ cups granulated sugar

3 tablespoons quick-cooking tapioca

¼ teaspoon nutmeg

Dash salt

3 cups ½-inch pieces fresh or frozen rhubarb (thawed)

2 cups sliced fresh strawberries

Pastry for a double-crust pie, preferably all-butter (recipe on
    page 51)

2 tablespoons butter

Preheat the oven to 375°F. In a small bowl, stir together the sugar, tapioca, nutmeg, and a dash of salt. In a large bowl, combine the rhubarb and strawberry pieces. Toss with the sugar and tapioca mixture to coat the fruit. Let the mixture stand for 15 minutes. Fill a pastry-lined 9-inch pie plate with rhubarb mixture. Dot with butter. Add the top crust. Seal and flute the edges, cutting decorative vents in the top. Cover the edge of your pie crust with a pie ring or aluminum foil and bake for 15 minutes; reduce heat to 350°F and continue to bake for 35 more minutes until the crust is golden brown and the juices are thickened and bubble slowly. Cool before cutting and serving.

Rhubarb Peach Pie

I think the combination of rhubarb and fresh peaches might be ingenious. The souring agent of rhubarb with fresh, sweet peach is a new favorite in my household. Since we raise happy bees and prefer honey to sugar, I substituted honey in this recipe to achieve a mellow sweetness that brings the flavors home.

Makes 1 pie, 6–8 slices

Pastry for a double-crust pie dough, preferably all-butter
    (recipe on page 51)
2½ cups ½-inch slices fresh or frozen rhubarb (thawed but
    not pressed)
2–3 large peaches (2½ cups fresh or frozen peach slices)
4 tablespoons all-purpose flour
¾ cup granulated sugar or ½ cup honey
1 teaspoon finely chopped, fresh-peeled ginger
Pinch salt
2 tablespoons butter, cut into small pieces
1 egg white beaten with 1 tablespoon water (optional)
Turbinado or other raw sugar for sprinkling on the top crust

Make the dough and refrigerate in two sections, covered, for 1 hour or more. If using frozen peach slices, do not thaw. If using fresh peaches, peel, pit, and cut the peaches in ¼-inch slices. The easiest way to peel peaches is to dip them in boiling water for 10 seconds, dunk them in an ice bath, then rub off the skins. If using frozen rhubarb, thaw the pieces in a colander but do not press.

Preheat oven to 425°F. Place peaches and sliced rhubarb in a large bowl. Toss with the flour. In another small bowl, combine the sugar or honey, ginger, and pinch of salt and mix well. Pour the honey mixture into the fruit, scraping the sides with a rubber spatula. Mix well. Place fruit mixture into the crust. Dot with butter. Remove the remaining dough from the refrigerator and roll out. Trim edges and crimp or flute them to seal. Cut several generous vents in the top crust. Brush egg-white wash across the pastry and sprinkle turbinado sugar over the top.

Bake the pie in the middle of the oven for 15 minutes. Reduce the oven temperature to 375°F, cover the edges of the crust with a pie ring or foil if desired, and bake for 50 minutes until the pie crust is golden brown and the juices are thickened and bubble slowly. Cool the pie before cutting and serving.

Sour Cream Rhubarb Pie with Meringue Topping

A meringue topping can't be beat in combination with rhubarb and sour cream. To make this, you'll want your egg whites to be at room temperature (no rushing!) and your beaters and bowls to be clean and dry. Two egg whites will give you moderate height. If you want a tall stunner, use three and up the sugar to 6 tablespoons, and the cream of tartar to ¼ teaspoon.

Makes 1 (9-inch) pie

Pastry for single-crust 9-inch pie, preferably all-butter (recipe on page 51)

1½ cups sliced fresh or frozen rhubarb (thawed)

2 egg yolks

1 cup granulated sugar

1 tablespoon all-purpose flour

1 cup sour cream

1 teaspoon cinnamon

Dash salt

Meringue topping:

2 egg whites

Dash salt

⅛ teaspoon cream of tartar

4 tablespoons granulated sugar

½ teaspoon vanilla

Preheat the oven to 400°F. Line the pie pan with the pastry. Spread the rhubarb over the top. In a bowl, beat the egg yolks and sugar, and then add the flour, sour cream, cinnamon, and salt. Mix well. Pour over the rhubarb. Bake for 10 minutes, then reduce the heat to 350°F and bake for 40 minutes more. While the pie is baking, in a mixing bowl, beat the egg whites and salt for 2 minutes. Continuing to beat, very gradually add the cream of tartar. The egg whites will be frothy with large bubbles along the sides of the bowl. Gradually add the 4 tablespoons of sugar while continuing to beat until the egg whites are stiff but still glossy. Add vanilla. Remove the pie from the oven and spread whipped meringue over the warm pie, going all the way to the edges to avoid shrinkage, creating decorative hillocks and dollops with the back of a spoon to your heart's content. Return the topped pie to the oven for 12 minutes. Remove, cool, enjoy!

Rhubarb Cream Pie

My husband's fond memories of his grandmother's rhubarb pie stem from summers on a 160-acre Nebraska farm. His German grandmother was a farmer's wife, and she made memorable afternoons anchored by pie. I have been in search of the rhubarb pie in his mind's eye by trial and error since the recipe is long lost. After testing this recipe, I'm getting closer, he says, as pieces are deftly removed to a plate and disappear.

Makes 1 pie, serves 6–8

2 cups ½-inch pieces fresh or frozen rhubarb (thawed)

⅔ cup granulated sugar

2 tablespoons all-purpose flour

⅛ teaspoon nutmeg

1 tablespoon water

½ teaspoon lemon flavoring

⅛ teaspoon red food coloring

1 (9-inch) unbaked pastry shell, preferably all-butter (recipe on page 51)

Cream filling:

1½ cups milk

¾ cup granulated sugar

3 tablespoons all-purpose flour

½ teaspoon salt

2 egg yolks (save whites for meringue)

Meringue topping:

2 egg whites

⅛ teaspoon salt

¼ cup granulated sugar

Preheat oven to 325°F. Mix together the rhubarb, ⅔ cup sugar, 2 tablespoons flour, and nutmeg. In a separate bowl, combine the water, lemon flavoring, and food color, and mix this with the fruit. Turn the combined fruit and flavoring mixture into the pastry-lined pan and bake for 40 minutes or until rhubarb is tender. Remove from the oven and cool.

As the pie is baking, heat the milk in the top of a double boiler. In a separate bowl, mix together the ¾ cup granulated sugar, 3 tablespoons flour, and ½ teaspoon salt and gradually pour this into the hot milk, stirring constantly, and cook until thickened. In a separate bowl, beat the egg yolks. Pour in a little of the milk mixture to combine, then gradually add the egg yolks into top of the double boiler. Continue to stir until eggs are cooked. Remove the double boiler from the heat, and cool. If needed, press the egg/milk mixture through a metal sieve with fine mesh to remove any bits of egg that did not blend well. Spread cooled cream filling over the rhubarb layer. For the topping, beat egg whites with the ⅛ teaspoon salt until stiff; very gradually beat in ¼ cup sugar. Spread meringue over the cream filling, being sure to go to the edges of the pie to avoid shrinkage. Bake pie at 350°F for 15 minutes more or until the meringue is golden brown. Cool before cutting so the layers hold together.

Double-Top Rhubarb Strawberry Cobbler

I first tasted this cobbler in New York State while visiting Lisa Engelbert at Engelbert Farms in Nichols, New York. The Engelbert family runs an organic dairy, with pleased cows, and a charming farm shop. Becky Blair, the farm baker, offered this Double-Top Rhubarb Strawberry Cobbler as the finishing touch on our visit. The room was cozy, and the group I was leading, chefs from Latin America, literally oohed and aahed over the welcoming food and atmosphere. The top layer of Becky's cobbler, with its special crunch, sets it apart. This is no soft-topped recipe with a bit of sprinkled coarse granulated sugar. It will feel a bit strange pouring boiling water over the layers, but don't hesitate. The unusual finishing crunch is perfection. Deep bow to Becky and to Lisa Engelbert for sharing. Five stars!

Makes 1 (9 x 13–inch) cobbler, often serves 10–12

Fruit:
4 cups fresh fruit (2 cups rhubarb, 2 cups strawberries)
¼ cup all-purpose flour
¼ cup granulated sugar
¼ teaspoon cinnamon

Batter:

2 cups all-purpose flour

1½ cups granulated sugar

½ teaspoon salt

6 tablespoons butter

1 teaspoon baking powder

1 cup milk

Topping:

1 cup granulated sugar

1 tablespoon all-purpose flour

¼ teaspoon salt

¼ teaspoon cinnamon

1 cup boiling water

Preheat oven to 350°F. Butter a 9 x 13–inch baking pan. In a large bowl, mix the rhubarb and strawberries, ¼ cup flour, ¼ cup sugar, and ¼ teaspoon cinnamon. Spread mixture in the 9 x 13–inch pan so the pan is half full. In a large bowl, combine all of the ingredients for the batter: flour, sugar, salt, butter, baking powder, and milk. Spread over the fruit mixture. In separate bowl, mix together all of the dry topping ingredients—sugar, flour, salt, and cinnamon. Spoon this over the batter. Pour the boiling water over the top of the mixture. Bake for 35–45 minutes until the top is golden brown. Serve with ice cream or whipped cream.

Rhubarb Strawberry Buckle

A buckle is a type of fruit cobbler that takes its name from its appearance: the dense batter sinks to the bottom of the pan as it bakes, which makes the streusel on top "buckle." This buckle, made even tastier with whipped cream dolloped on top of a warm serving, is simple to make, with no rolling pin needed.

Makes 9 squares

Topping:
⅓ cup all-purpose flour
⅓ cup packed dark brown sugar
½ teaspoon cinnamon
4 tablespoons chilled unsalted butter, sliced

Batter:
6 tablespoons unsalted butter, softened
½ cup granulated sugar
1 large egg
1 teaspoon vanilla
½ cup sour cream
1¾ cups all-purpose flour
2 teaspoons baking powder
Pinch of salt
¾ cup hulled and sliced fresh strawberries
¾ cup ½-inch pieces fresh or frozen rhubarb (thawed)
Heavy cream for serving

Preheat oven to 375°F. Butter an 8 x 8–inch square pan. In a small bowl, prepare the topping—combine the flour, dark brown sugar, and cinnamon for the topping. Cut in 4 tablespoons butter with a pastry blender or fork until it resembles coarse crumbs. Set aside.

In a large mixing bowl, beat 6 tablespoons butter until creamy to prepare the batter. Gradually beat in the sugar until light and fluffy. Add the egg and vanilla and beat until smooth. Add the sour cream and mix until blended. In a medium-sized bowl, combine the flour, baking powder, and salt. Quickly stir the dry ingredients into the butter and sour cream mixture to just moisten. The batter will be thick and lumpy.

Gently fold in the strawberries and rhubarb and turn into the prepared pan. Crumble the topping over the batter. Bake 30–35 minutes or until a toothpick inserted in the middle comes out clean. Cool on rack for 15–20 minutes. Cut into 9 squares and serve warm with heavy cream or a dollop of slightly sweetened whipped cream.

BLUEBERRY VARIATION: Substitute ¾ cup blueberries for the ¾ cup strawberries.

Rhubarb Apple Crumble

Here's another version of cobbler named for its appearance. The classic crumble top with rhubarb and apple fruit underneath is a winner. One of my favorite things to do in the spring during rhubarb season is to walk through our farmers' market and imagine possible combinations of berries and rhubarb, or fruits like apple and rhubarb. You make this recipe by tossing the fruit with a little sugar and sweet spices; spreading it in a baking dish; scattering a hand-crumbled mixture of flour, other grains or nuts, sugar, and butter over the top; then baking the whole thing until the juices are bubbly and the top is crunchy.

Serves 8

3 cups fresh or frozen rhubarb

3 cups peeled and diced apple

1¼ cups granulated sugar

¼ cup + 1 cup all-purpose flour

1 teaspoon vanilla

¼ teaspoon ground cardamom

½ teaspoon salt

1 cup dark brown sugar

8 tablespoons cold butter, cubed

Preheat the oven to 375°F. In a medium-sized bowl, mix together the rhubarb, apple, sugar, ¼ cup of flour, vanilla, and cardamom. Spread the rhubarb-apple mixture into a 9 x 13–inch baking dish.

To make the topping, add the remaining 1 cup flour, the dark brown sugar, and salt to a medium-sized bowl. Then add the butter. Mix using your fingers until the mixture resembles coarse crumbs. Spread the topping over the fruit and bake for 35–45 minutes, or until the filling is bubbly and the topping is lightly browned. Let cool for 20–30 minutes before serving. Serve with ice cream or whipping cream.

VARIATIONS: Alternative fruit, like strawberries, can replace the apples. If the fruit is sweet, decrease the granulated sugar to 1 cup.

Rhubarb Crisp

For the cobbler lovers who prefer a bit of crunch, this crisp is for you. The oats, brown sugar, and butter do the heavy lifting with the unbeatable flavor of rhubarb rounding out each bite. Add some vanilla ice cream and you'll be a forever fan.

Serves 4–6

1½ cups sifted all-purpose flour

1 cup dark brown sugar

1½ cups old-fashioned oats

¾ cup melted butter

1 teaspoon cinnamon

4 cups ½-inch pieces fresh or frozen rhubarb (thawed)

1 cup granulated sugar

1 cup water

1 teaspoon vanilla

2 tablespoons cornstarch

Preheat oven to 350°F. In a large bowl, mix flour, dark brown sugar, oats, butter, and cinnamon together until crumbly. Press all but ½ cup into the bottom of a 9 x 9–inch pan. Arrange the rhubarb over the flour mixture. In a saucepan, combine sugar, water, vanilla, and cornstarch, and cook on medium heat until liquid is clear; pour mixture over the rhubarb. Top with remaining ½ cup of crumbly mix. Bake 1 hour.

Rhubarb Betty

Cobblers, crumbles, and crisps are made from a layer of fruit with either a streusel or pastry topping, but a betty is different. I was skeptical of this 1903 recipe from J. E. Morse's book *The New Rhubarb Culture* but loved it after making it. It resembles a bread pudding, with crispy bread bits to crunch into on the top, and can be served with hard sauce (secret sauce, I should say!) or butter. It's a great way to use up bread and it's quick to mix up. You can use leftover cake crumbles instead of bread for a decadent alternative. A traditional betty is made by three alternating layers of fruit and crumbs.

Serves 6

1 cup granulated sugar

1 teaspoon nutmeg

1 teaspoon salt

2 cups water

4 cups breadcrumbs or torn small pieces of dry bread

2 cups ½-inch pieces fresh or frozen rhubarb (thawed)

3 tablespoons butter

Preheat oven to 350°F. In a small bowl, mix the sugar and nutmeg and set aside. In a wide bowl, add salt to the 2 cups of water and stir to dissolve. Add the bread pieces to the salted water for about 30 seconds. Lift the soaked bread pieces out of the water with a slotted spoon, squeezing a little of the salted water out if needed so it is moist but not soupy. Layer the soaked bread in a 9 x 5–inch bread loaf pan, alternating with about a third of your rhubarb, and a third of the sugar and nutmeg mix. You should be able to make 2–3 layers, ending with bread at the top. Dot the top with butter and bake until golden brown, about 45 minutes. Serve with butter and sugar or hard sauce.

Hard sauce:
1 stick softened butter
1½ cups powdered sugar
2 tablespoons whiskey (or to taste)

Beat butter in a mixing bowl until light yellow and fluffy. Add the powdered sugar until incorporated. Add the whiskey and mix well. Serve warm over Rhubarb Betty or other desserts such as pie. Can be stored covered tightly with plastic wrap for one week.

Rhubarb Cream Cheese Glacé

This dessert has a cream cheese layer that pulls all the flavors together into a delicate and pretty tart. I use a tart pan with removeable sides to make things easier to cut, but you can make it work without. The crust is buttery and light. The cream cheese layer is slightly sweet, and it's topped by unsweetened rhubarb and then a sweetened glaze. Would be lovely served with tea or coffee or for after dinner to accompany pleasant conversation at the table.

Serves 8

1 cup all-purpose flour

½ cup chopped pecans

½ cup (1 stick) butter, softened

2 cups chopped fresh rhubarb

1 cup + ⅓ cup water

1 cup granulated sugar

3 tablespoons cornstarch

1 (8-ounce) package cream cheese, softened

1 cup powdered sugar

½ cup hulled and sliced strawberries

Whipped cream or ice cream, for serving (optional)

Preheat oven to 350°F. In a mixing bowl, combine the flour, pecans, and butter. Press the flour mixture into a 9-inch tart pan with removeable sides, or a 9-inch glass pie plate. Bake for 15 minutes. Remove from oven and cool.

While the crust is cooling, bring rhubarb and 1 cup of water to a boil, then turn down the heat to medium-low and simmer for 15 minutes. Turn off the heat and set aside.

To make a glaze, separate ⅓ cup of the rhubarb into a small pan. In a small bowl, blend granulated sugar, cornstarch, and the ⅓ cup water, and add this to the rhubarb pan. Bring to a boil. Continue to boil one minute, stirring constantly. Strain this glaze mixture into a bowl through a mesh sieve, pushing slightly with the back of a spoon. Spread cream cheese over the bottom of the cooled crust. Spread the unsweetened rhubarb mixture over the cream cheese. Arrange the strawberry slices in decorative rounds in the middle, and cover the entire tart with the sweetened glaze. Refrigerate 2 hours or until firm. Serve with whipped cream or ice cream.

All-Butter Pastry

I learned from master pie baker and writer Kate Lebo that an all-butter crust makes the pie. I've made butter crust and crust with vegetable shortening. I've made it with butter and shortening combined, with a mix of nut flours, and I've been known to add whiskey. But this, using good butter and good flour like King Arthur—this is the best.

Makes 1 double crust

2 ½ cups all-purpose flour   1 cup chilled unsalted butter

1 tablespoon granulated sugar   ½ cup ice water (approximately)

1 teaspoon salt

In a large bowl, mix the flour, sugar, and salt. Cut the butter into pieces and add into the flour mixture. Using a pastry cutter or your fingers, work the butter into the flour until it resembles coarse crumbs. Start by drizzling ¼ cup of the cold water around the bowl. Toss to distribute the moisture. Then, add more water a little at a time, working the dough with your hands, until the dough holds together and is slightly tacky. Gather the dough into 2 balls and form thick disks using your hands. Wrap each disk with plastic wrap and refrigerate for 1 hour or more before rolling.

quick breads, muffins, scones, pancakes + cakes

Rhubarb Muffins

I love a good muffin with my morning tea. This love started young. Muffins may have been the first recipe I learned to bake in my home economics class in seventh grade—I can picture it: the muffin tins, the ovens we made faces across to tease each other, the aroma, and the triumph twenty minutes later. The addition of rhubarb in this recipe gives each bite a surprising lift not found in those basic muffins. You may find you needed that lift all along.

Makes 10–12 muffins

1 cup ½-inch pieces fresh or frozen rhubarb (thawed), cut in
    half down the center of the rib
¼ cup water
1¾ cups all-purpose flour
½ cup granulated sugar
2½ teaspoons baking powder
½ teaspoon salt
1 beaten egg
½ cup milk
⅓ cup cooking oil

Preheat the oven to 400°F. In a small saucepan, heat the rhubarb and ¼ cup water to boiling. Turn down the heat and simmer for about 8 minutes or until the rhubarb is soft when pressed with a fork. In a large bowl, stir together the flour, sugar, baking powder, and salt. Make a well in the center. In a separate bowl, combine the egg, milk, and oil. Fold the egg mixture and softened rhubarb all at once into the flour mixture. Stir until just moistened; the batter will be lumpy. Grease muffin cups or line with paper baking cups; fill ⅔ full. Bake for 20–25 minutes or until golden. Remove from pans; serve warm.

Crumble-Top Oatmeal Rhubarb Muffins

A streusel topping for muffins? Bring it on! These disappear very quickly in my house. The muffin has a good crumb, and the top is satisfying. Great with coffee. Put them out on the counter and see how fast they go.

Makes 24 muffins

Crumble topping:

¼ cup all-purpose flour

¼ cup old-fashioned oats

2 tablespoons dark brown sugar

1 teaspoon cinnamon

¼ cup unsalted butter, chilled

Muffins:

1½ cups all-purpose flour

1¼ cups dark brown sugar

1 cup old fashioned oats

1 teaspoon baking soda

1 teaspoon salt

1 cup buttermilk, or 1 cup whole milk + 1 teaspoon vinegar

1 teaspoon vanilla extract

½ cup vegetable oil

1 egg

2 cups finely chopped fresh or frozen rhubarb (thawed)

Rhubarb sugar sprinkle (optional):

1 teaspoon turbinado or other raw sugar

⅛ cup finely chopped fresh or frozen rhubarb (thawed)

Preheat the oven to 350°F.

To make topping: combine the flour, oats, dark brown sugar, and cinnamon in a small bowl. Dice the butter and, using a pastry cutter or fork, cut the butter into the dry ingredients until it resembles rough crumbs. Set aside in the refrigerator.

To make the muffins: In a large bowl, combine the flour, 1¼ cups dark brown sugar, oats, baking soda, and salt. Mix to blend. In a small bowl, combine the buttermilk, vanilla, oil, and egg. Whisk together. Add the milk mixture to the flour mixture until just combined. Fold in the rhubarb. Fill paper-lined muffin cups ¾ full. Add crumble topping to fill. Sprinkle the top with small bits of rhubarb and turbinado granulated sugar, if desired. Bake at 350°F until firm, 25–30 minutes. Serve warm with butter.

Rhubarb Quick Bread

This would make the perfect mini loaf for gifting at the holidays. But, then again, I make this as a full 9 x 5–inch loaf and it gets eaten pronto. It has loft, great texture, and flavor. Enjoy it warmed up the next day for breakfast. A friend likes to toast pieces the morning after it's made and has been known to slather butter on it, too.

Makes 1 loaf, 12 slices

1 large egg
1 cup buttermilk, or 1 cup whole milk + 1 teaspoon vinegar
½ cup vegetable oil
1 cup granulated sugar, + 1 tablespoon for sprinkling
2 teaspoons vanilla
1 tablespoon baking powder
½ teaspoon salt
2 cups all-purpose flour
2 cups diced fresh or frozen rhubarb, thawed

Preheat oven to 350°F. Spray and line a 9 x 5–inch loaf pan with parchment paper. In a large bowl, whisk together egg, buttermilk, oil, granulated sugar, and vanilla until smooth. Add baking powder and salt, then fold in the flour, taking care not to overmix. Fold in the rhubarb. Using a rubber spatula, spread the mixture into the loaf pan. Smooth top. Sprinkle 1 tablespoon of sugar evenly over the surface of the batter. Bake for 60–65 minutes, or until firm when lightly touched on top and a toothpick inserted near the center comes out without raw batter. Cool for 15 minutes, then remove from pan to cool on a cooling rack. If you are not using parchment paper, let the bread cool in the pan.

VARIATION: Add ¾ cup chopped pecans to the batter.

Rhubarb Scones

Let me just say, adding rhubarb to the perfection of a breakfast scone turned out brilliantly. In fact, let me just brush the crumbs off the page for you right now and go make another batch.

Makes 8 scones

2 cups all-purpose flour
½ teaspoon salt
1 tablespoon baking powder
½ cup granulated sugar
5⅓ tablespoons cold unsalted butter
1 large egg, beaten
½ cup + 2 tablespoons heavy whipping cream
¾ cup fresh rhubarb, or frozen rhubarb, thawed, sliced into
    ½-inch pieces, and then cut in half down the center of the rib
Turbinado or other raw sugar for sprinkling

Preheat the oven to 400°F. Grease or use parchment paper to prepare a baking sheet. Combine the flour, salt, baking powder, and sugar in a large bowl. Cut in the butter with a pastry blender or fork until the mixture resembles coarse crumbs. Mix in the egg and cream until just combined. Stir in the rhubarb. Turn the dough out onto a lightly floured surface. Gently knead 5–6 times or until dough just comes together. Shape dough into an approximate 8-inch circle. Place on a prepared baking sheet and cut into 8 wedges. Sprinkle with turbinado sugar, if desired. Bake for 20–25 minutes, or until edges start to turn light golden brown. Remove to a wire rack to cool. Serve warm or at room temperature, adding butter or jam, if desired. Store leftovers in an airtight container.

Rhubarb Pancakes

Often on Sunday mornings, my husband can be found humming softly as he stirs up a bowl of batter and proceeds to flip cakes. When our children were young, they would often try to speed up the process by helping butter the warm pancakes while he continued his steady pace. Here, I've tried to re-create the magic of those special mornings by adding a little rhubarb to the mix.

Makes 8–10 (4-inch) pancakes

1 cup finely chopped fresh or frozen rhubarb (thawed)
¼ cup water
Zest of half a lemon
½ cup + 1 tablespoon granulated sugar
1 cup flour
2 teaspoons baking powder
¼ teaspoon salt
1 egg, beaten
1 cup milk
2 tablespoons cooking oil
¼ teaspoon cinnamon mixed with ½ teaspoon granulated
    sugar (optional)

In a saucepan, add the rhubarb pieces, ¼ cup of water, lemon zest, and ½ cup sugar. Cook until the rhubarb softens but retains its shape, about 5 to 6 minutes. Drain and set aside. In a large bowl, mix the flour, 1 tablespoon sugar, baking powder, and salt. Push the dry mixture to the sides of the bowl, making a well with the back of your spoon. In a separate bowl, mix the egg, milk, and oil. Add the rhubarb pieces. Pour the wet ingredients and rhubarb all at once to the flour mixture. Stir until just moistened; do not over stir. Pour ¼ cup of batter onto a hot, lightly greased griddle or skillet. Cook about 2 minutes until you see bubbles pushing through to the surface. Using a spatula, flip the pancake and cook for about 2 minutes on the other side. Remove to a plate and butter and sprinkle with cinnamon and granulated sugar mixture, if desired. Serve warm.

Rhubarb, Apple, and Walnut Coffee Cake

The walnuts and apple pair well with rhubarb in this coffee cake. Sprinkle a generous amount of turbinado or other raw sugar on top for a little extra pizzaz. In a surprising twist for most baked goods, this recipe gets better the next day. If using frozen rhubarb for this recipe, be sure to measure it out while still frozen, then thaw completely in a colander. Do not press the liquid out.

Makes 1 loaf, 12 slices

2 large eggs
¾ cup granulated sugar
¼ cup vegetable oil
½ teaspoon vanilla
1½ cups all-purpose flour
2¼ teaspoons baking powder
½ teaspoon salt
½ teaspoon cinnamon
¾ cup chopped peeled apple
¾ cup chopped fresh or frozen rhubarb (thawed)
½ cup chopped walnuts
Turbinado or other raw sugar to sprinkle on top

Preheat oven to 350°F. In a large bowl, whisk eggs, sugar, oil, and vanilla until blended. In another bowl, whisk flour, baking powder, salt, and cinnamon; add the dry mixture to the egg mixture and stir just until moistened. Fold in apples, rhubarb, and walnuts. The batter will be thick. Transfer to into a greased 8½- or 9-inch loaf pan. Sprinkle a generous amount of turbinado sugar over the top. Bake 50 minutes or until a toothpick inserted in center comes out clean. Cool in pan 10 minutes before removing to wire racks to cool.

Easy Rhubarb Buttermilk Cake with Cream Cheese Icing

Sometimes you just need a little cake but don't have time for an elaborate confection. I feel you. This delightful recipe is not time-consuming and will fit the bill. You can serve it plain, but I give my thumbs up to a cream cheese frosting made with rhubarb simple syrup.

Makes 1 (9 x 9–inch) square cake, serves 9

2 cups thinly sliced fresh or frozen rhubarb, thawed and cut in half down the center of the rib

2 cups all-purpose flour

½ cup unsalted butter at room temperature

1 cup granulated sugar, + 2 teaspoons for sprinkling

1 large egg at room temperature

1½ teaspoons vanilla

2 teaspoons baking powder

1 teaspoon salt

½ cup buttermilk

Preheat oven to 350°F. Lightly butter a 9 x 9–inch baking pan or line it with parchment paper. In a medium-sized bowl, add 1 tablespoon of the flour to the sliced rhubarb and toss to coat. Set aside. In a mixing bowl, cream the butter and granulated sugar until it becomes pale yellow and fluffy. Beat in the egg and vanilla. In a separate bowl, mix the remaining flour, baking powder, and salt. Add half the flour mixture to the bowl with the butter and mix well, alternating with the buttermilk twice. Blend until just combined, not overmixing. Fold in the rhubarb with a spatula. The batter will be thick. Spread the batter into the prepared pan and sprinkle the top with 2 teaspoons granulated sugar. Bake for 40–45 minutes, or until golden and a knife inserted in the center comes out clean. Let cool before icing with cream cheese rhubarb icing (below). Great served with coffee or with ice cream.

Cream cheese rhubarb icing:
3 ounces cream cheese, softened
4 tablespoons butter, softened
2 cups powdered sugar
2–3+ tablespoons rhubarb simple syrup (recipe on following
    page) or fresh orange juice
1 teaspoon orange zest, if using orange juice instead of
    rhubarb syrup

Mix the cream cheese and butter until well blended. Add the powdered sugar, mix, and add rhubarb syrup until spreading consistency, about 2 tablespoons. Alternatively, use 2–3 tablespoons fresh orange juice and 1 teaspoon orange zest.

RHUBARB SIMPLE SYRUP: Boil together: 1 cup water, 1 cup sliced rhubarb, and ½ cup granulated sugar for about 15 minutes. Strain through a wire strainer, using the back of a spoon to squeeze the rhubarb juice from the pulp. Pour into a glass jar and cool. Use to mix up rhubarb cream cheese icing and/or refreshing drinks.

Upside Down Rhubarb Cake

The bottom of this upside-down cake, which ends up being the top, has a sweet crispy tang that pairs wonderfully with the soft cake. Once flipped, the topping soaks through and makes each bite a delight, maybe especially with coffee. Use a cast-iron skillet to bake if you can flip it easily when hot. Otherwise, a 10-inch cake pan works as well. For a thicker cake, use a 9-inch pan, being careful the ingredients don't spill over the top before baking. Make sure to test that the cake is well cooked with a toothpick before removing it from the oven. The pink rhubarb will marble all the way through once flipped. Underdone cake will crumble under the weight of the topping.

Serves 6–8

3 cups fresh or frozen rhubarb sliced in ½-inch pieces

1½ cups granulated sugar, divided

2 tablespoons + 1½ cups all-purpose flour

½ teaspoon ground nutmeg, divided

½ cup butter, melted, divided

2 large eggs, room temperature

2 teaspoons baking powder

¼ teaspoon salt

⅔ cup milk

Whipping cream, beaten and sweetened (optional)

Preheat oven to 350°F. Place rhubarb in a greased cast-iron skillet, a cake pan, or a springform pan. In a small bowl, combine ¾ cup of the sugar, 2 tablespoons of the flour, and ¼ teaspoon nutmeg and sprinkle over the rhubarb. Drizzle with ¼ cup of melted butter.

For the cake, mix the remaining ¼ cup melted butter and ¾ cup sugar until well blended in a mixing bowl. Add the egg. Combine the remaining 1½ cups flour and ¼ teaspoon nutmeg, baking powder, and salt and gradually add this to the egg mixture, alternating with milk. Beat well after each addition. The batter will be silky and thick. Spread over the rhubarb. Bake about 35–40 minutes or until a toothpick inserted in the middle comes out clean. Make sure the cake is cooked through so it holds up after it is flipped. Remove the cake from oven and loosen its edges with a knife. Invert the cake immediately onto a serving dish. Serve warm. Top with whipped cream if desired.

Rhubarb Swirl Cheesecake

Taking inspiration from Sara Bir in *The Pocket Pawpaw Cookbook*, I swirled rhubarb curd into my favorite cheesecake. Creamy cheesecake plus a tart swirl of pink rhubarb—a kiss your fingertips moment!

Makes 1 (9-inch) cheesecake, serves 8–10

Crust:
1¼ cups graham cracker crumbs
3 tablespoons granulated sugar
⅓ cup butter, softened

Cheesecake, first layer:
2 (8-ounce) packages cream cheese, softened
¼ cup granulated sugar
2 eggs
1 teaspoon vanilla
1 cup rhubarb curd (recipe on page 130)

Cheesecake, second layer:
1 pint sour cream
⅓ cup granulated sugar
1 teaspoon vanilla

Preheat oven to 350°F. In a medium-sized bowl, mix together the graham cracker crumbs, 3 tablespoons sugar, and butter. Reserve ¼ cup of crust mixture in a bowl and set aside. Press the remaining crust mixture into a 9-inch pie pan and bake for 10 minutes. Remove from oven and cool for 5 minutes, then place in the refrigerator. In a mixing bowl, whip together the cream cheese, ¼ cup sugar, eggs, and 1 teaspoon vanilla. Spoon onto the cooled crust. Tap pan on countertop to remove air pockets. Spoon dollops of the rhubarb curd randomly over the cream cheese mixture. Drag a knife through the dollops two or three times (at most) to make your swirl. Return to the oven and bake for 15 minutes. Remove from oven and cool for 5 minutes. In a small bowl, mix the sour cream, ⅓ cup sugar, and 1 teaspoon vanilla. Gently spread the sour cream mixture over the baked mixture and return to the oven for another 10 minutes. Sprinkle the reserved graham cracker mixture over the top. Chill well before slicing.

cookies

Rhubarb Shortbread

I bake shortbread with pecans. I bake shortbread with lemon zest. I bake shortbread plain or with pecans and lemon and dip them in chocolate. Does there need to be a shortbread intervention, you ask? Wait and taste this version first. By using rhubarb curd (recipe on page 130) to make a shortbread sandwich cookie, the buttery taste of the pastry combines with the tartness of rhubarb in an exceptional way.

Makes 1 (9 x 9–inch) square, 15 pieces

8 tablespoons unsalted butter
1 cup granulated sugar
1 large egg
1 teaspoon lemon zest
Juice of half of a large lemon
2 cups all-purpose flour
⅛ teaspoon salt
1 teaspoon baking powder
½ cup rhubarb curd (recipe on page 130)

Preheat the oven to 350°F. Butter or line a 9 x 9–inch square baking dish with parchment paper. Cream the butter and sugar in a mixing bowl until the sugar is dissolved and the mixture is light and fluffy. Beat in the egg. Add the lemon zest and lemon juice. Gradually add the flour, salt, and baking powder. The dough will be stiff. Using your hands, spilt the dough in half and make 2 balls. Press 1 ball into the bottom of the prepared pan, pressing dough to the edges. Spread the rhubarb curd over the top of the base layer of shortbread. On a clean work surface or parchment paper, press the second ball of dough into roughly the size of the 9 x 9–inch baking dish. Carefully lift the dough and place it on top of the rhubarb layer. Gently pat the dough in place. Bake for 12 minutes or until the edges are slightly brown. Cool before cutting.

Rhubarb Strawberry Jam Thumbprints

There is something happy about jam-print cookies. They feel a little old-fashioned, a little perfect, like there should be a doily under the plate. The rhubarb strawberry jam adds color and taste to the buttery base.

Makes 48 cookies

¾ cup butter, softened
½ cup granulated sugar
2 eggs
1½ teaspoons vanilla
2 cups all-purpose flour
1½ teaspoons baking powder
¼ teaspoon salt
½ cup rhubarb strawberry jam (recipe on page 121)
⅓ cup chopped hazelnuts (optional)

Cream the butter and sugar in a mixing bowl. Add the eggs and vanilla; beat well. In a separate bowl, combine the flour, baking powder, and salt. Gradually add the flour mixture to the butter mixture. Mix well. Chill for at least 1 hour.

Preheat oven to 350°F. Grease two cookie sheets. Shape the cookie dough into 48 balls and place them 2 inches apart on the cookie sheets. Using a moistened finger, make an indentation on each ball. Spoon ½ teaspoon of the rhubarb strawberry jam, mixed with the chopped hazelnuts if using, into each indentation. Bake for 10–13 minutes. Cool on racks and store in airtight containers.

Rhubarb Almond Bars

In the past, I have made this recipe with apricot preserves, but I am a changed woman now. Rhubarb preserve, with its tart-sweet taste, offers a striking contrast to the buttery comfort of the shortbread base and avoids being cloyingly sweet. The almond topping, especially when hot out of the oven, is light on the tongue. Best eaten the day they are made.

Makes 24 pieces

1 cup butter
1 cup powdered sugar
2 cups flour
2 cups diced fresh or frozen rhubarb (thawed)
1 cup + ¾ cup granulated sugar
2 tablespoons cornstarch
¼ cup water
3 egg whites
¾ cup almond flour or finely ground nuts

Preheat oven to 350°F. In a large bowl, mix butter, powdered sugar, and flour until well blended. Press mixture into a 9 x 13–inch pan and bake for 10 minutes. Cool. In the meantime, in a medium-sized pan, cook the rhubarb, 1 cup granulated sugar, cornstarch, and ¼ cup water over medium heat for 10 minutes until thickened and bubbly, adding 1 tablespoon of water if needed. Spread rhubarb mixture over the cooled crust. Next, beat the egg whites until stiff, gradually adding in the remaining ¾ cup granulated sugar. Add the almond flour. Mix well and spoon to cover the rhubarb layer. Bake for 20–30 minutes until golden brown. Cut into squares while warm.

mains

Pork Tenderloin Medallions with Rhubarb–Black Pepper Relish

The combination of the tart flavor profile of rhubarb and the spiciness of black pepper works well with rich meats. Try it with pork tenderloins and see if you don't agree.

Makes enough for 4 servings

1 pound pork tenderloin
½ teaspoon salt
¼ teaspoon black pepper
2 teaspoons vegetable oil
1–2 cups Rhubarb–Black Pepper Relish (recipe on page 137)

On a cutting board, use a sharp knife to cut the tenderloin into 8 slices. Lay plastic wrap over the slices and use a meat mallet, your palm, a rolling pin, or a wine bottle to gently pound each slice into ½-inch thickness. Season each piece with salt and pepper. Heat oil in a skillet, and add the pork to the pan in a single layer (do this in batches if needed) to quickly sear the tenderloin slices, about 2–3 minutes each side (until the internal temperature is 145°F). Set the pork aside on a covered plate to keep warm. To serve, arrange the pork medallions on 4 serving plates and spoon the Rhubarb–Black Pepper Relish over the top.

Rhubarb Blueberry Barbecue Baked Beans

You won't miss the bacon or other meats in this baked bean dish! The Rhubarb Blueberry Barbecue Sauce is rich and tasty enough to make believers out of a family of farmers in Missouri. I feel sure it will do the same for you. The flavor profile is medium spiciness, full of tangy and sweet fruity notes.

Makes 10–12 servings

1 pound dry beans—navy, pinto, great northern, or a mix of
    beans (our preference)
2 teaspoons salt
¼ teaspoon baking soda
2 cups Rhubarb Blueberry Barbecue Sauce (recipe on page 141)

To prepare the beans, pour the dry beans into a large pot and cover them by at least 2 inches with cold water. Cover the pot and soak the beans overnight, or for at least 12 hours. Drain the beans. Cover them with fresh water by about 2 inches and stir in the salt and baking soda. Bring the pot of beans to a boil, then reduce heat to low and simmer for 1 hour, stirring occasionally. Drain the beans.

To prepare the baked beans and sauce, preheat oven to 350°. Add the beans to a Dutch oven or a deep oven-safe dish with a lid. Stir in the Rhubarb Blueberry Barbecue Sauce to cover. Cover the pan and bake for 1 hour. Check the beans and add a little water if they are looking dry. Bake for another 30 minutes. Remove lid and bake for a final 30 minutes to thicken. Stir and serve warm.

Rhubarb Blueberry Barbecue Country-Style Ribs

The Rhubarb Blueberry Barbecue Sauce is equally good with country-style pork ribs as it is with baked beans and was taste-tested faithfully and often. Rhubarb with meat turns out well in almost all instances, and this recipe is no different.

Serves 4–6

4 teaspoons Creole seasoning, *or*

      1½ teaspoons salt

      1 teaspoon coarsely ground pepper

      1 teaspoon garlic powder

      ½ teaspoon cayenne

3 to 4 pounds boneless country-style pork ribs

1+ tablespoons oil

2 cups Rhubarb Blueberry Barbecue Sauce (recipe on page 141)

Preheat oven to 325°F. Rub Creole seasoning into ribs. Refrigerate, covered, while preparing sauce. In a Dutch oven, heat 1 tablespoon oil over medium heat. Brown ribs in batches, adding more oil as needed. Add Rhubarb Blueberry Barbecue Sauce to the pan, turning the ribs to coat. Bring to a boil. Cover and place in the warm oven; bake until ribs are tender, about 2 hours. The last 30–35 minutes, bake uncovered until sauce is slightly thickened.

Lamb or Beef Stew with Rhubarb

We often think of rhubarb as something for pie and cobbler and other desserts. But its first culinary use may have begun along the Silk Road trade routes and predates uses of sugar to sweeten the end result. The routes of traders in the Silk Road era, 130 BCE to 1453 CE, moved through Central Asia, an area known for its uses of herbs, its interest in meats, and its rhubarb—which merchants helped naturalize in Europe and beyond. Here, adapted from Laura Kelley's lamb-rhubarb dish in "Rhubarb's Silk Road History" on *The Silk Road Gourmet*, this stew shows Central Asian influence. Persians and others have long understood the use of rhubarb in savory dishes like lamb stew. And though using rhubarb in stew is tricky, as this tender vegetable falls apart after just a few minutes of cooking, it is superb as a souring agent to complement earthy meats. Be sure to cook all other ingredients almost completely, including the meat, before adding rhubarb for the best results. The mint here, though only ¼ cup, deeply flavors the dish.

Serves 4

2 tablespoons peanut oil
1 pound lamb roast or beef
    sirloin cut into 1-inch cubes
1 large onion, peeled and thinly
    sliced into crescents
3 teaspoons garlic, peeled and
    diced
4 dried hot red chili peppers
1 teaspoon salt
1 teaspoon black pepper

1 cup water

1 cup beef or chicken stock

2 teaspoons grated nutmeg

¼ cup chopped fresh mint (or more, to taste)

1 medium bunch fresh cilantro, chopped

1½ tablespoons granulated sugar (or more, to taste)

3 cups 1-inch slices fresh or frozen rhubarb

Heat oil in a medium saucepan. When hot, sear lamb or beef cubes over high heat until golden brown around the edges, stirring constantly. When meat is browned, remove from the pan with a slotted spoon and set aside. Lower heat to medium, and in the same pan, add the onions, sautéing until they start to soften. Add the garlic, chili peppers, salt, and pepper and stir until the garlic starts to turn golden brown at its edges. Next, add water and beef or chicken stock, and when hot, add lamb back into the pot. Add 1 teaspoon of the grated nutmeg to the stew. Cover and cook over low heat for 1 hour, stirring occasionally, until lamb or beef becomes tender.

When the lamb or beef is nearly done, add the chopped mint and stir well. Then add the cilantro and sugar and stir in as well. Cook for another 3 to 5 minutes and then add the rhubarb and cook another 3 to 5 minutes or until the rhubarb softens but is still firm. Remove from heat, grate the remainder of the nutmeg in, and serve. Serve over rice, or cooked barley or millet works well, too.

Rhubarb Tagine with Chickpeas

If you are a fan of chickpeas, you will love this lip-smacking main or side dish inspired by the blog *Alison's Allspice*. The dates and rhubarb combine unexpectedly well, with tangy, fruity results.

Serves 4

3 tablespoons olive oil

2 medium onions, chopped

2 garlic cloves, sliced

1 teaspoon minced ginger

1 cinnamon stick

½ teaspoon cumin seeds

¼ teaspoon cayenne pepper

1 (14-ounce) can diced tomatoes

2 (14-ounce) cans chickpeas, rinsed and drained
    (option: soak 1 cup dried beans overnight and simmer for
    30 minutes)

¼ cup chopped dates

1½ cups chopped fresh or frozen rhubarb

1½ cups vegetable broth

Black pepper to taste

1 tablespoon honey or dark brown sugar

½ cup minced fresh parsley, for garnish

In a large saucepan, heat the oil on high heat. Add the onion, turn the heat to low, and sauté for about 8 minutes, or until the onion is translucent. Add garlic, ginger, cinnamon stick, cumin seeds, and cayenne and stir for 1 minute. Add the tomatoes, and continue to cook for 2 minutes. Add the chickpeas, dates, rhubarb, broth, and black pepper. Let this simmer on low heat for 15 minutes with the lid off or until the liquid cooks down by ¾. Stir in the honey or dark brown sugar. Garnish with parsley. Serve with couscous or with a toasted baguette.

VARIATION: Substitute 14 ounces tofu for the chickpeas.

Rhubarb-Glazed Ham

Next time you bake a ham, choose one of the tangy rhubarb sauces, such as Rhubarb Blueberry Syrup or the Easy Rhubarb Sauce, in this book to finish it. The word to describe the result? Pizzazz!

Serves 20

1 fully cooked smoked whole ham, 10–12 pounds
½ cup Easy Rhubarb Sauce (recipe on page 140) or
    Rhubarb Blueberry Syrup (recipe on page 147)

Preheat oven to 325°F. Remove fat on ham in excess of a ¼-inch layer. Score the fat with a sharp knife in a 2-inch diamond pattern. Place ham in a roasting pan and bake, uncovered, until the internal temperature of the meat reaches 140°F, about 2½ to 3 hours. Spread half of the sauce over the ham and bake an additional 15 minutes. Spread the remaining sauce over the ham and bake another 15 minutes until the glaze is set and the ham is browned.

Rhubarb Chutney Ketchup and Lamb Meatballs

Chef Barbara Sibley of the wonderful La Palapa restaurant in New York City makes this recipe with lamb meatballs as an appetizer at home holidays. Barbara has a way with food, so I didn't hesitate to try this out. This sauce has a piquant kick and robust flavor. Excellent as sauce with the lamb meatball recipe below, on pork chops, or alongside grilled chicken. It would be an exciting ketchup with bratwurst. It won't last long.

Makes 2 cups of Rhubarb Chutney Ketchup Sauce

1½ tablespoons olive oil

¼ cup coarsely chopped onion

⅛ cup chopped garlic (about ½ a head)

¼ cup balsamic vinegar

⅛ cup red wine vinegar

⅛ cup honey, or ¼ cup dark brown sugar

1 teaspoon cinnamon

½ tablespoon red pepper flakes

½ teaspoon paprika

¼ teaspoon black or white pepper

½ teaspoon salt, or to taste

2½ cups fresh or frozen rhubarb, chopped coarsely

Heat the oil in a large skillet. When hot, sauté the onions and garlic until the onion is translucent and the garlic edges just begin to brown. Add the vinegars, dark brown sugar or honey, cinnamon, red pepper flakes, paprika, black or white pepper, and salt. Once the dark brown sugar is dissolved, add the rhubarb and cook until tender, about 10 minutes. Adjust seasoning to taste. Remove from heat and allow to cool. Puree using an immersion blender or remove the mixture to a blender.

Lamb Meatballs
Makes about 16 meatballs

1 pound ground lamb
2 tablespoons thick plain
    yogurt
1 tablespoon minced fresh
    garlic
½ teaspoon salt

½ teaspoon black pepper
1 teaspoon onion powder
1 teaspoon ground cumin
½ cup chopped fresh cilantro
2 tablespoons olive oil

In a medium bowl, combine the ground lamb, yogurt, garlic, salt, black pepper, onion powder, ground cumin, and cilantro. Using a tablespoon, measure one heaping tablespoon per meatball onto a plate until all of the meat is used, approximately 16 meatballs. With wet hands for easier handling, shape each portion into a round meatball. Heat the olive oil in a large skillet over medium-high heat until it shimmers and becomes fragrant, for about 2 minutes. Add the meatballs in a single layer and cook them, turning frequently until golden brown, for about 5 minutes, reducing the heat to medium as needed. Add ¼ cup of water to the bottom of the skillet. Cover and cook the meatballs until they are cooked through, about 2–3 more minutes. Using a slotted spoon, remove the meatballs from the skillet to a serving dish. Add the Rhubarb Chutney Ketchup. Serve immediately.

Gingery Beef Curry with Rhubarb

This recipe is inspired by Anglo Indian tradition and usually uses tamarind instead of rhubarb. Rhubarb may be handier, and it adds the proper tart taste to the dish. Most meats work with this recipe—beef, pork, mutton, lamb, or venison. It's spicy, tart, and rich; opt out of the two dried red chilies if you prefer, but keep the cayenne. The dish is best with a balance between the tart and piquant.

Serves 4–6

1 pound beef sirloin, stew meat, or other meat of your choice
    cut into 1-inch cubes
¼ teaspoon cayenne
½ teaspoon coriander powder
½ teaspoon cumin powder
1 teaspoon salt
3 tablespoons vegetable oil
1 (3-inch) cinnamon stick
5 whole cloves
¼ teaspoon peppercorns
2 medium onions, cut in half and thinly sliced into half-moon
    shapes

2 dried red chilies, broken

1 tablespoon ginger-garlic paste, or 1 teaspoon garlic and
    1 teaspoon fresh ginger, mashed

3 tablespoons tomato paste, half a 14-ounce can of tomato
    puree, or 2 medium tomatoes chopped

¾ cup 1-inch slices fresh or frozen rhubarb

½ cup water

2 potatoes, peeled, boiled, and cut into quarters (optional)

In a large bowl, add meat, cayenne, coriander, cumin, and salt. Mix well and set aside to marinate. Heat the oil in a large pan. Add the cinnamon stick, whole cloves, and peppercorns. Fry for 20 seconds and add the onions. Add the dried red chilies. Continue to stir and fry until the onions just begin to brown, about 10 minutes. Add the marinated meat. Stir well and cook until the meat is browned, about 10 minutes. Add the ginger/garlic and mix well. Add the tomato and stir. Add just enough water to cover the meat mixture in the pan. At this point, cover and simmer until the meat is tender, about 1¾ hours, or pressure cook for 15 minutes. (If using a pressure cooker, once done, add meat mixture to a large pan and bring to a boil for 10–15 minutes, until the sauce reaches half of its original liquid.)

While the meat is cooking, in a separate pan, heat ½ cup water and rhubarb to boiling. Keep at a hard simmer for 8–10 minutes. When the rhubarb is very soft, mash it with a potato masher or a fork. Set aside. When the curry is finished cooking, add in the rhubarb and bring to a boil. Add potatoes if using. Turn down the heat and simmer 3–4 minutes. Let rest 15–20 minutes before serving. Serve over rice or with Indian breads.

Rhubarb Chicken Stew with Cauliflower

This dish is balanced beautifully, with honey and savory stock alongside the trademark slightly tart taste of rhubarb. My family all had seconds and thirds until the pan was completely cleared. I added cauliflower for a bit of a crunch, but if you are a potato fan, they would work here, too.

Serves 4–6

2 tablespoons vegetable oil

6 boneless skinless chicken thighs

1 large onion, cut in half and thinly sliced

5 garlic cloves, finely chopped

2 tablespoons olive oil

1 heaping teaspoon black pepper

1 teaspoon turmeric

1 (14-ounce) can diced tomatoes (or 2 fresh, medium-sized
    tomatoes, chopped)

5 tablespoons honey

3 tablespoons fresh lime juice

2 cups ½-inch slices fresh or frozen rhubarb

2 cups large cauliflower florets

3 cups chicken stock

Salt to taste, if stock is not salted

Heat the oil in a large pan with at least 2-inch sides, add the chicken pieces, and fry for 5 minutes. Turn the chicken over and fry another 5 minutes. Cut chicken into large pieces, if preferred. Remove the chicken from the pan and set aside. Add the onions into the same pan. Cook 3 minutes. Add the garlic. Continue to cook 2 minutes, stirring often. Add black pepper, turmeric, and chopped tomatoes and cook for 2–3 minutes. Add the honey, lime juice, and chopped rhubarb. Return the chicken to the pan and add chicken stock. Bring to a boil, then reduce heat to low and cook for 10 minutes uncovered. Add the cauliflower florets and cook for an additional 30 minutes, uncovered, stirring occasionally. Adjust salt, honey, and lime juice to taste. Serve with biscuits or a toasted baguette and butter.

VEGAN AND VEGETARIAN OPTION: Replace chicken with 14 ounces of tofu cut into squares and pan fried. Replace chicken stock with vegetable stock.

Coconut Green Curry with Chicken and Rhubarb

Coconut milk makes this dish slightly sweet, and the tart-savory components round out the palate-pleasing taste.

Serves 4

1 pound boneless dark chicken or breast meat

3 cloves garlic, minced

¼ teaspoon cayenne pepper

1-inch piece of fresh ginger, mashed

2 tablespoons white wine vinegar

2 tablespoons green curry paste

2 tablespoons vegetable oil

1 medium onion, cut in half and in half again, then sliced into
    half-moon shapes

1 green pepper, sliced

2 cups ½-inch slices fresh or frozen rhubarb

4 ounces fresh mushrooms, sliced

1 tablespoon honey

2 tablespoons raisins

1 (14-ounce) can coconut milk

1 teaspoon salt

¼ teaspoon additional cayenne, or to taste (optional)

Cut the chicken into 1-inch pieces. In a large bowl, mix the chicken pieces, garlic, cayenne, and ginger. Add the vinegar and green curry paste and mix well. Cover and set aside for 1–2 hours.

In a large skillet, heat the oil and add the onion and green pepper. Stir and fry for 2 minutes. Add the rhubarb and mushrooms and sauté for 2 minutes. Stir in the honey. Remove the pan from the heat.

In another pan, add the marinated chicken and cook pieces for 2–3 minutes, separating the chicken into 2 batches if needed. When the chicken begins to brown, add the rhubarb mixture to the chicken, then add the raisins and the coconut milk. Add the salt and additional cayenne, if desired. Reduce the heat to low and simmer for 10 minutes until the sauce is slightly thickened and the chicken is cooked through. Serve with rice.

VARIATION: For a vegetarian/vegan option, substitute 14 ounces pan-fried tofu for the chicken.

Red Lentils with Spinach and Rhubarb (Dal)

Dal is a comfort food for me—and this dish made with red lentils cooks up quickly and satisfies hunger and comfort needs quite handily. Adding rhubarb gives the flavor profile a lift in liveliness. This 30-minute recipe offers an alternative to meat-based protein and will engage all the taste buds!

Serves 4

1 cup red lentils

½ inch fresh ginger, peeled and finely chopped

½ teaspoon turmeric

1 teaspoon salt

1 cup ½-inch slices fresh or frozen rhubarb

2 cups fresh spinach, cut into short strips

3 tablespoons vegetable oil or ghee

½ teaspoon cumin seeds

2 garlic cloves, minced

½ onion, thinly sliced

½ teaspoon cayenne

¼ cup plain yogurt (optional)

2 tablespoons chopped cilantro leaves (optional)

Salt to taste

Wash lentils in two to three changes of water. Place the lentils into a deep saucepan and fill it ⅔ full with water. Heat to boiling, then turn down to a hard simmer on medium heat. Add the ginger and continue to simmer. Using a large spoon, skim the foam that will accumulate on the surface and dispose. You may need to do this 3–4 times until there is no more excess foam. Add the turmeric, salt, and rhubarb. Continue to simmer, stirring occasionally, for about 25 minutes. Add water as necessary. The lentils will be the consistency of a thick soup and will not hold their shape. Once the lentils are at this stage, add the spinach. Let simmer.

While the lentils and spinach are finishing, in a separate small pan, heat the oil or ghee. Once hot, add the cumin seeds, garlic, and sliced onions. When this mixture just begins to brown, add the cayenne and immediately lift the pan off the heat. Pour this tempering mixture over the lentils. Deglaze the pan with a little of the thickened lentils. Adjust salt to your taste. Serve hot with rice. Top with a spoon of yogurt and cilantro, if desired.

VARIATION: Add 1 medium potato cut into small ½-inch cubes to the lentils during the last 15 minutes they are boiling. Or, fry 4 or 5 small pieces of cauliflower in vegetable oil until their edges are slightly brown. Add these into the dal.

Yellow Lentils with Rhubarb

Since lentils are a weekly event at our house, I was instantly intrigued by Najmieh Batmanglij's Braised Rhubarb with Herbs and Saffron in the book *Silk Road Cooking*. I decreased the mint, added just a little more chili, and dropped the chives (since I never seem to have them on hand). It makes a wonderful soup, if you happen to have leftovers.

Serves 4

4 tablespoons vegetable oil

1 sweet onion, thinly sliced

5 cloves garlic, roughly chopped

2 serrano chilies, seeded and finely chopped

2 cups chopped parsley

¼ cup chopped mint

½ cup chopped dill

½ cup chopped cilantro

⅔ cup yellow split peas, picked over and washed

Salt and pepper to taste

¼ teaspoon turmeric

3½ cups vegetable stock or water

1 fresh tomato, quartered

Pinch of saffron soaked in 2 tablespoons hot water

Juice of half a lime

2 tablespoons granulated sugar

3 cups 1-inch or smaller chunks of fresh or frozen rhubarb,
(thawed)

Heat the oil in a large pot and add the onion. Sauté 3–4 minutes or until translucent, then add the garlic, chilies, parsley, mint, dill, and cilantro. Mix well. Add the split peas, salt, pepper, turmeric, and the stock or water. Bring to a boil, then cover and simmer 35 minutes or until the split peas have softened, adding more water as needed. Add the tomato, the saffron and its soaking liquid, the lime juice, and sugar. Bring back to a boil, then arrange the rhubarb on top. Cover and simmer another 10–15 minutes until the rhubarb is soft. Taste and adjust salt or sugar as necessary. Delicious served over couscous or rice or with plenty of bread and alongside lamb or chicken.

Keema with Rhubarb
(Minced Beef with Peas and Rhubarb)

I grew up eating my mother's northeast Indian keema with peas or sometimes small cubes of potato as a comfort food, so I wasn't sure I wanted to mess with a classic. It turns out, I do. In India, it might be made with minced lamb or sometimes with ground beef. Here, I use beef, peas, and rhubarb. Great with paratha bread or with rice.

Serves 4–6

2 tablespoons vegetable oil

1 bay leaf

5 whole cloves

5 whole cardamom pods

1 dried red chili

1 (3-inch) cinnamon stick

1 large onion, finely chopped

3 cloves of garlic, minced

1 pound minced meat

2 Roma tomatoes, quartered

½ cup frozen peas, thawed

¾ cup ½-inch slices fresh or frozen rhubarb (thawed)

½-inch piece of fresh ginger, peeled and finely chopped
¼–½ teaspoon cayenne
¼–½ teaspoon garam masala (optional)
1 teaspoon salt, or to taste

Heat the oil in a deep, large saucepan. When hot, add the bay leaf, cloves, cardamom, dried chili, and cinnamon stick. Let the whole spices sizzle for 10 seconds, then add the onion. Stir and fry the onion until the edges just begin to brown, about 4–5 minutes. Add the minced meat and stir and fry until the meat is fully browned, about 3 minutes. Add the tomato and continue to cook for 1 minute. Add the peas and rhubarb. Stir well. Add the ginger, cayenne, and salt. Reduce heat to low, add ½ cup water, cover, and simmer until the rhubarb loses its shape, about 8 minutes. Remove the lid, then stir and fry for 1–2 minutes to thicken slightly. Add garam masala if desired. Adjust salt. If desired, remove whole spices. Serve with rice or Indian paratha breads. Tasty served with chutney or yogurt sprinkled with chopped cilantro.

Beef or Vegetable Pot Pie with Rhubarb

At the farm, we often needed filling and fast meals before our growing children went out to various sports practices, theater practices, or just out to roam the farm after homework. Since both of us were working, a pot pie often served us well—it was quick, warm, filling, and everyone loved it. It was also a great way to use up the vegetables in the refrigerator—confession, my recipe was a bit of a changeling, depending on the week and what was in the vegetable drawer. I also often reduced the meat (or eliminated it) and added more vegetables just because I preferred it that way. It would be equally as good as a true vegetable pot pie. Here, I've taken my farm recipe and tweaked the flavors with rhubarb in a way that brings out the yum.

Serves 4

2 tablespoons vegetable oil
1 onion, chopped
1 pound ground beef
2 stalks celery, chopped
1 bay leaf
½ teaspoon black pepper
⅛ teaspoon cayenne

2 teaspoons good quality beef
	or vegetable bouillon or
	soup base
1 tablespoon ketchup
½ cup green peas
1 cup peeled and julienned
	carrots

1 medium potato, peeled and cut into ½-inch cubes

1 cup ½-inch slices fresh or frozen rhubarb (thawed)

1–2 tablespoons cornstarch stirred into ½ cup water

Salt if needed (note: soup base is often pre-salted)

Pastry for top

Preheat oven to 350°F. In a large, deep pan, heat the vegetable oil and fry the onions until they begin to soften. Add the ground beef and stir until cooked through. Add the celery, bay leaf, black pepper, cayenne, beef or vegetable bouillon or soup base, ketchup, peas, carrots, potato cubes, and rhubarb. Stir and fry until well blended. Add water to just cover and let simmer for 5 minutes. Stir the cornstarch in a ½ cup of water and pour into the simmering mixture to your preferred thickness. Pour the beef and vegetables in its sauce into an oven safe dish or Dutch oven. Place the pastry (see recipe on page 51) across the top of the dish, crimping the edges to seal. Cut vents into the top of the crust with a knife. Bake for 30 minutes or until the crust is golden brown.

SUGGESTION: If using the pastry recipe in this book, which makes enough for two crusts, use your second dough ball for a single crust pie for dessert! Or wrap it well and freeze for use within two weeks.

refreshing
drinks

Rhubarb Mint Lemonade

There's not much better on parched days than a refreshing sour lemonade made from rhubarb. You can store rhubarb-mint syrup in the refrigerator for a week, or it can be frozen for a month so it'll be ready for you when you need it.

Makes 6 servings

2–3 tablespoons Rhubarb Mint Simple Syrup (recipe on page 144)
Ice cubes
Sparkling water
Fresh mint, for garnish (optional)

Pour 2–3 tablespoons of the simple syrup in the bottom of 6 (8-ounce) glasses. Add ice and sparkling water. Serve. Garnish with fresh mint if desired.

Rhubarb Lassi

Cooling yogurt makes this drink the best refreshment. While you may have tried a plain lassi or one made with mango, rhubarb adds a nice lifting taste to the drink. Not as thick as you sometimes find in US restaurants, this version is light on the tongue and full-on summer in the mind.

Serves 4

1 cup fresh or frozen rhubarb
1 tablespoon water
2 cups plain yogurt
1 cup ice
1 cup sparkling water
3 tablespoons granulated sugar
½ teaspoon ground cardamom or ground cumin
Toasted almonds, for sprinkling (optional)

In a small pan, heat the rhubarb and 1 tablespoon of water until boiling. Turn down the heat and simmer for 5 minutes until the rhubarb is soft, adding a little water if needed. Remove from heat and cool for 3–4 minutes. Place the rhubarb, yogurt, ice, sparkling water, and ground spices in a blender. Mix well and serve over ice. Sprinkle toasted almonds over the top, if desired.

Refreshing Rhubarb Spritzer

Sometimes you just need a spritzer, and rhubarb makes a snappy, refreshing one. Such a pretty pale pink in the glass, too.

Makes 8 servings

1 cup sliced fresh or frozen rhubarb
¾ cup granulated sugar
½ cup water
1 tablespoon fresh lemon juice
3 cups seltzer or dry sparkling wine like prosecco or cava, chilled
Grapefruit and/or lemon slices (optional)

In a small saucepan, stir rhubarb, granulated sugar, water, and lemon juice over medium heat. Bring the mixture to a boil, then reduce the heat to medium low and simmer until the rhubarb loses all structure and the sugar dissolves, about 10–12 minutes. Strain through a fine mesh sieve, pressing the solids with the back of a spoon to extract as much liquid as possible and then discarding them. Cover and refrigerate the syrup until cold, 2 hours or more. Divide the syrup among 8 glasses with ice. Top with seltzer or sparkling wine. Garnish with lemon and grapefruit slices, if you like, and serve immediately.

Rhubarb Lemon Fizz

You might not yet be aware, but an uplifting rhubarb fizz has already earned a place at your table—or deck, as the case may be. This bubbly vodka fizz will help you sit back and enjoy the day one sip at a time.

Makes 1 drink

2 ounces vodka
2 tablespoons Rhubarb Simple Syrup (recipe on page 143)
1 tablespoon fresh lemon juice
2 ounces club soda or dry sparkling wine such as cava or prosecco
Lemon wheel, for garnish (optional)

Add the vodka, 2 tablespoons of the rhubarb simple syrup, and lemon juice to a cocktail shaker and fill with ice. Shake vigorously, then strain into a glass filled with fresh ice. Top with club soda or sparkling wine and garnish with a lemon wheel, if desired.

Rhubarb Gimlet

Rhubarb also plays well with gin, if that's your cocktail preference.

Makes 1 drink

2 ounces rhubarb gin
¾ ounce Rhubarb Simple Syrup (recipe on page 143)
¾ ounce fresh lime juice

Mix the gin, simple syrup, and lime juice in a shaker filled with ice. Strain and pour into a glass with fresh ice cubes.

NOTE: if using gin unflavored with rhubarb, boil ½ cup fresh or frozen rhubarb in 2 tablespoons of water for 10 minutes. Strain liquid through a sieve and discard the remaining solids. Add 1½ tablespoons (¾ ounce) of this unsweetened liquid to the drink ingredients above.

Rhubarb Punch

Sailors are said to have first encountered punch in the early seventeenth century. The original drink in the Indian subcontinent was called *paanch*, which comes from the Hindi word *pāñch*, meaning "five." The drink was often made with five ingredients: some combination of alcohol, sugar, juice, water, and spices. The sailors from the British East India Company used local ingredients such as arrack, rum, fruit, and spices including nutmeg and mace. I enjoy the slightly sweeter taste of pineapple and substituted it for the lemon juice found in LaDonna M. Thompson's 1980 recipe in *Rhubarb Cooking for All Seasons*.

Makes 30 drinks

4 cups finely cut fresh or frozen rhubarb

10 cups water

3½ cups granulated sugar

2 cinnamon sticks

24 whole cloves

2 cups orange juice

1 cup pineapple juice

1 cup lime juice

1 teaspoon vanilla

In a saucepan, bring the rhubarb and 2 cups water to a boil over medium heat. Turn down the heat and cover. Simmer for 10 minutes. Remove from heat and cool. Blend in a blender and set aside in a large bowl. Next, in a saucepan, simmer 2 cups water, sugar, and spices, covered, for 10 minutes. Strain out the spices and add the liquid to the rhubarb mixture. Add the orange, pineapple, and lime juices, vanilla, and 6 cups cold water to the bowl. Pour into a punch bowl over ice. Serve cold.

Strawberry Rhubarb Daiquiris

There is really nothing better for some of us than a sweetly pink drink. Even better, add a smidge of white rum and, by all means, a tiny umbrella. Cheers!

Makes 1 drink

1½ ounces white rum
1 ounce Strawberry Rhubarb Simple Syrup (recipe on page 145)
1 tablespoon fresh lemon or lime juice
Wheel of lemon or lime, for garnish (optional)

Combine rum, Strawberry Rhubarb Simple Syrup, and lemon or lime juice in a shaker with ice. Shake vigorously. Strain into a glass filled with ice.

FOR FROZEN STRAWBERRY RHUBARB DAIQUIRIS: Add rum, Strawberry Rhubarb Simple Syrup, lemon/lime juice, and a pinch of coarse salt to a freezer-safe container or zipper-lock bag. Freeze for about 8 hours. When ready to make your drink, blend 8 ice cubes, or the equivalent in crushed ice, and the daiquiri mix from the freezer in a blender. Blend until ice is uniform. Adjust with more Strawberry Rhubarb Simple Syrup if needed. Garnish as preferred.

jams,
chutneys +
preserves

Simple Rhubarb Jam

This tasty, easy-to-make jam is a pretty red and is tart and sweet. If using frozen rhubarb for this recipe, measure it out while still frozen, then thaw completely in a colander. Do not press the liquid out.

Makes about 2 cups

3 cups granulated sugar
½ cup cold water
4 cups ½-inch slices fresh or frozen rhubarb

In a saucepan, bring the granulated sugar and water to a boil for 4–5 minutes, stirring as needed. Add the rhubarb and let simmer 8 minutes, or until the rhubarb is very soft and loses its shape. The jam will be lumpy; press mixture with a fork or mash large pieces with a potato masher to make a smoother jam, if desired. Pour the mixture into a sterilized jar. Jam will thicken as it cools. Refrigerate, freeze, or process for canning. Rhubarb jam perfectly accompanies scones, biscuits, and toast.

Rhubarb Strawberry Jam

This classic pairing works well for jam, too, not just pies—the sweet strawberries work in tandem with the rhubarb to create a taste explosion on the tongue.

Makes about 2 cups

1 cup 1-inch pieces fresh or frozen rhubarb
1 cup hulled and sliced fresh strawberries
½ cup water
1½ cups granulated sugar

Mix rhubarb, strawberries, water, and sugar in a saucepan; cook over medium heat, stirring often, until the rhubarb is very tender and loses its shape, about 12 minutes. The jam will be lumpy; press mixture with a fork or mash large pieces with a potato masher to make a smoother jam, if desired. Pour mixture into a sterilized jar. Cool. Refrigerate until ready to use.

Rhubarb Marmalade

Marmalade always makes me think of my dad. He never ate a lot of sweets, but he could not resist orange marmalade. I can still see him sneaking extra spoons for his toast, munching happily while sipping tea on a weekend morning. When I saw this recipe, I confess it was the orange rind that got my attention. This pretty, deeply red-orange rhubarb marmalade recipe is a tweaked version of the one in the 1980 cookbook *Rhubarb Cooking for All Seasons*, and it spins me into memories.

Makes 1½ cups

½ cup water
1 orange, very thinly sliced, and then cut in half
1 lemon, very thinly sliced, and then cut in half
2 cups ½-inch pieces fresh or frozen rhubarb
2 cups granulated sugar
1 tablespoon minced ginger root

Remove seeds from the orange and lemon. Add ½ cup water to a saucepan, add the fruit and peel, and simmer for 1 hour, covered. Add a little water if needed. Take off the heat and add the rhubarb and the sugar. Add the ginger and let stand, covered, for 24 hours.

Heat the saucepan over medium-high heat and bring the mixture to a boil. Reduce the heat to low and cook until thick and syrupy, about 35 minutes, stirring so it does not burn. The marmalade will darken to a deep reddish-orange toward the end of the cooking time. When the mixture sheets from the spoon, remove from heat and pour into sterilized glass jars. Best used within two weeks and stored in the refrigerator or preserved by canning for gifting or for longer storage.

TIP: When I made this marmalade the first time, it turned out too hard and tacky. I did not simmer the rind beforehand and overcooked the jam in the effort to soften it more. I have since discovered an easy fix: If your jam turns out hard and tacky, it was cooked over too hot a burner and/or for too long (my error). Spoon the overcooked jam into a large saucepan. Add 1 cup of water and bring the mixture to a boil over medium heat, stirring to incorporate all of the water. Cook until the gelling point has been reached (217°F to 221°F, depending on how fluid you like it). Spoon into clean jars and process in a water bath if you are canning.

Rhubarb Orange Preserve/Relish

When I realized I could add pieces of orange peel to a rhubarb concoction at any time, it was an "Aha!" moment for me. In 1903, J. E. Morse in *The New Rhubarb Culture* mentioned putting rhubarb-orange preserves into a "preserving kettle" and later canning the results in glass jars with sealed lids. I made refrigerator preserve to perk up my morning instead. This recipe is more relish-like than jammy and good as a side relish for meats but still tasty on toast.

Makes about 4 cups

6 large thin-skinned oranges, peeled, cut in pieces, and
    seeds removed
Peels of 3 of the oranges, cut into very thin strips
3 cups ½-inch slices fresh or frozen rhubarb
3½ cups granulated sugar

Place the orange fruit, strips of peel, rhubarb, and sugar in a crock or other non-metallic bowl, cover, and let stand for 8 hours. Pour the mixture into a large saucepan and cook over medium heat, stirring often, until thickened, about 7 minutes. Immediately pour into glass jars with lids, cool, and store in the refrigerator for one month, or freeze.

Rhubarb Fig Jam

Adding small bits of candied orange peel makes this an irresistible, thick, figgy jam with a rhubarb base. If you like, double the recipe ingredients and can this jam for later use or for gifts. Otherwise, refrigerate once cool and eat within the 2–3 weeks. Fair warning: it's very addictive.

Makes about 2 cups

4 cups 1-inch slices fresh or frozen rhubarb
¼ pound dried figs, shredded in a food processor
1 cup granulated sugar
¼ pound candied orange peel, cut into small pieces

Mix the rhubarb, figs, and sugar in a large glass jar or crock. Cover and let stand for 8 hours. Place mixture in a large cooking pot and bring to a boil, stirring often, then turn down the heat to very low and simmer for 50 minutes, stirring occasionally. The mixture will be very thick. Stir in the candied orange peel. Remove from heat and pour the jam into either a large glass jar with a lid or prepared jars for canning.

Rhubarb Apricot Jam

Apricot and rhubarb play well together—and make a pretty jam for gifting. Great as an eat-now refrigerator jam, but super for canning to bring sunshine to your table in winter.

Makes about 5 cups

6 cups 1-inch slices fresh or frozen rhubarb
3 cups granulated sugar
4 fresh apricots, skins removed, pitted and chopped

Mix the rhubarb and sugar in a large bowl, cover, and let stand for 8 hours. Place mixture in a large saucepan, add the apricots, and bring to a boil. Once boiling, reduce heat to a hard simmer, stirring often, for 10–12 minutes. Remove from heat and spoon jam into sterilized jars or freezer containers. Cool completely. Best used within 2 weeks stored in the refrigerator, freeze for up to 2 months, or preserve by canning.

VARIATION: Use 4 ripe peaches in place of the apricots.

Rhubarb Apple Chutney

I'm all about chutney and often make simple versions to go alongside meals. Though made from apples and rhubarb, fruit my mother didn't consider, this dish is spiced like her signature tomato chutney, and I highly recommend it.

Makes about 2 cups

1 tablespoon vegetable oil
1 teaspoon black or brown
    mustard seeds
1 dried red chili
2 cups 1-inch slices fresh or
    frozen rhubarb
2 apples, peeled, cored, and
    chopped

¾ cup granulated sugar
2 tablespoons golden or
    black raisins, according to
    preference
¼ to ½ teaspoon cayenne
¼ cup fresh lemon juice

Heat oil in a deep saucepan. Once hot, add the mustard seeds and dried chili and let sizzle for 5 seconds. Add the rhubarb and stir and fry for 2 minutes. Add the apples. Fry for 2 minutes. Reduce heat to low and add sugar, raisins, and cayenne. Simmer for 15 minutes or until apples are tender but still hold some of their shape. Remove from the heat. Stir in lemon juice. Spoon into a sterilized glass jar, cover, and store in the refrigerator for up to 2 weeks.

Spiced Rhubarb Apricot Chutney

This recipe makes a very thick chutney that is not hot (pungent) but sweet-tangy to taste. It's flavored with ginger, cinnamon, and cloves to create a rich side for any type of meal. Delicious alongside pork or on your holiday table.

Makes about 3 cups

1 tablespoon vegetable oil
1 (2-inch) cinnamon stick
1 tablespoon chopped fresh
    ginger
6 whole cloves
1 medium onion, chopped
2 large cloves garlic, chopped

1 pound fresh or frozen
    rhubarb (about 4 cups), cut
    into ½-inch slices
1 cup chopped dried apricots
1 cup granulated sugar
⅓ cup fresh lemon juice
1 cup golden raisins
Pinch salt

Heat the oil in a large saucepan. Add the cinnamon stick, ginger, and cloves, and let sizzle for 10 seconds. Add the onion and garlic. Stir and fry for 2 minutes. Add the rhubarb, apricot, sugar, lemon juice, and raisins. Continue to stir over high heat. When the liquid in the pan begins to boil, lower the heat to low and cook for about 10 minutes or until the apricots are soft and the sauce is thickened. Refrigerate before serving.

Rhubarb Ginger Chutney

Gingery rhubarb chutney balances the flavors in your meal deliciously. Use it as a palate cleanser alongside meats and vegetarian fare.

Makes about 1 cup

1 tablespoon vegetable oil
½ dried red chili
3 cardamon pods
1 (2-inch) cinnamon stick
1 medium onion, finely
　 chopped
1½ cups 1-inch slices fresh or
　 frozen rhubarb

1-inch piece of fresh ginger,
　 or ¼ cup finely chopped
　 candied ginger
¼ cup fresh lemon juice
⅓ cup granulated sugar
Pinch salt

Heat oil in a medium saucepan. When hot, add the dried chili, cardamon, and cinnamon stick. Stir and fry for 10 seconds. Add onion, rhubarb, and ginger. Stir well. Add the lemon juice, sugar, and salt. Decrease heat to medium-low, leave uncovered, and simmer for 15 minutes or until the mixture is no longer watery. Stir occasionally. Store in a glass jar in the refrigerator for up to 2 months.

Rhubarb Curd

You've heard of lemon curd—that fabulously tart, sweet fruit filling often used in delicate desserts—but did you know you can make it with rhubarb? Curds have a satiny feel in the mouth like nothing else. Add the flavor of rhubarb and you have a winning combination. I began with a lemon curd recipe I've had tucked away for years and folded in strained rhubarb instead of lemon juice.

Makes about 2 cups

2 cups ½-inch slices fresh or
    frozen rhubarb (thawed)
¼ cup water
1 cup granulated sugar
Juice of 1 lemon

4 large eggs, beaten
1 or 2 pinches of ground
    freeze-dried strawberries
    for pink color, if desired
6 tablespoons unsalted butter

In a blender, add the rhubarb and water and process until very smooth. Press the puree through a fine mesh sieve with the back of a spoon, discarding the solids. You should have about 1 cup of juice. Put the juice into a saucepan along with the sugar and lemon juice and stir until blended.

In a separate bowl, whisk the eggs. Add the eggs to the saucepan and, stirring constantly, bring the mixture to a simmer on medium heat. If desired, grind a few freeze-dried strawberries in a spice grinder and add their fine powder to the mixture in the saucepan to reach your desired pink color. Continue to simmer until the mixture comes to a boil and thickens so it coats the back of a spoon, about 10 minutes. Remove from heat, add the butter in pieces, stirring well between each addition until they melt. Pour the curd through a mesh strainer to remove any bits of cooked egg, and fill clean jars. Curd will thicken more as it cools. Cool to room temperature, then refrigerate overnight. Use in Rhubarb Swirl Cheesecake (recipe on page 71) or for other delights. Best if used within 2 weeks.

syrups, sauces + relishes

Rhubarb Salsa

For a lively salsa that is great with tacos or burritos and on chips: add rhubarb!

Serves 10

2 cups very thinly sliced fresh rhubarb, rotated and cut in half down the center rib

2 teaspoons dark brown sugar

4 tablespoons lime or lemon juice

1 small onion, roughly chopped

1 green bell pepper, seeded and quartered

1 yellow bell pepper, seeded and quartered

1 serrano pepper (or more, to taste), seeded and roughly chopped

½ cup fresh cilantro leaves

3 Roma tomatoes, quartered

1½ teaspoons salt

¼ teaspoon garlic powder

Black pepper to taste

Bring a large pot of water to a boil. When hot, add the rhubarb and stir for 20 seconds. Drain the rhubarb into a colander and rinse it with cold water; drain again. Transfer the rhubarb to a large bowl.

In a small bowl, dissolve the dark brown sugar in the lime or lemon juice. Set aside.

In a food processor, pulse the onion, green, yellow, and serrano peppers, and cilantro 3 or 4 times to finely chop; add these to the rhubarb bowl. Add the tomatoes, then the dark brown sugar and lime mixture. Add salt, garlic powder, and black pepper. Stir. Refrigerate for 3 hours to blend flavors.

Rhubarb Pickles

These are simple, quick refrigerator pickles that are tart and a bit crunchy. Let the pickling liquid cool slightly before pouring it over the rhubarb to keep the optimum crunch. I make them with champagne vinegar, but rice vinegar, apple cider vinegar, or white balsamic also work. You can use different aromatics as you like. I used star anise here, but tarragon, lemongrass, or ginger would be a good pairing, too.

Makes 2 cups

1½ cups thinly sliced (to ¼-inch or less) fresh rhubarb
1 cup champagne vinegar
¼ cup granulated sugar
2–3 star anise, or a sprig of another aromatic such as
    tarragon or lemongrass, or 1 garlic clove

Divide the rhubarb in 2 (8-ounce) glass jars, or 1 (16-ounce) glass jar. In a small saucepan, heat the vinegar and sugar. Once the sugar has dissolved, remove from heat, add the aromatic of your choice, and let cool for 3-4 minutes. Pour over the rhubarb, leaving about 1 inch of headspace. Cover with a lid and refrigerate. Once cooled, can be eaten right away. Best within 3 weeks.

Rhubarb–Black Pepper Relish

Oregon chef Stephanie Pearl Kimmel uses this relish with duck. With slight adjustments to her recipe, I suggest it with pork medallions (recipe on page 82).

Makes enough for 4 servings

2 cups chicken stock, reduced to ½ cup

⅔ cup granulated sugar

2 cups ½-inch slices fresh or frozen rhubarb (thawed)

1 large shallot, thinly sliced

Zest from one half of a lemon

1 tablespoon white wine vinegar

½ tablespoon black peppercorns, coarsely ground

1 tablespoon butter

Salt to taste

In a small saucepan, heat the chicken stock on medium-high until it reduces to ½ cup. Set aside.

In a medium saucepan, add the sugar and heat over medium heat until it begins to caramelize, stirring and watching closely so it does not burn. Add the rhubarb, shallot, and lemon zest and stir to coat all the ingredients with the caramelized sugar. Reduce the heat to medium-low and add the vinegar and black pepper. Add the reduced chicken stock and stir. Continue to simmer the mixture until the rhubarb is soft, about 8 minutes. Remove from heat and add the butter. Salt to taste.

Rhubarb Ketchup with Blueberries

A surprising relish for burgers or any other dish you want to liven up. Sweet and spicy!

Makes about 1½ cups

2 cups finely chopped fresh or frozen rhubarb
1 large onion, finely chopped
¾ cup white vinegar
½ cup water
2 cups blueberries, or substitute strawberries or mixed berries

1¼ cups dark brown sugar
½ teaspoon ground cinnamon
½ teaspoon ground allspice
½ teaspoon ground cloves
½ teaspoon black pepper
¼ teaspoon cayenne
⅛ teaspoon ground nutmeg
1 teaspoon sea salt

In a deep pan, mix rhubarb, onion, vinegar, and water and cook over medium heat for about 30 minutes, stirring occasionally. Remove pan from heat and add the blueberries or other berries, dark brown sugar, cinnamon, allspice, cloves, black pepper, cayenne, nutmeg, and salt. Stir until well blended. Return the pan to the stove and cook over low heat for about 1 hour, stirring occasionally. Cool, cover, and store in the refrigerator. Best used within a week. Or, freeze for up to 1 month.

Easy Rhubarb Sauce

The tangy-sweet flavor profile of this simple sauce is so versatile that it makes a great accompaniment to meat, and it can be added to a dessert such as ice cream or pound cake.

Makes about 2 cups

4 cups ½-inch slices fresh or frozen rhubarb
⅓ cup granulated sugar
⅛ teaspoon cinnamon
Pinch of salt

In a large saucepan, combine the rhubarb, sugar, cinnamon, and salt. Heat to boiling, then reduce heat, cover, and simmer about 8 minutes. Cool to room temperature, then refrigerate. Best used within 2 weeks.

Rhubarb Blueberry Barbecue Sauce

A unique barbecue sauce so good you'll want it on your table whenever you can. Though the recipe might look long, it's a snap to make and uses items usually found in your pantry. This sauce is excellent with baked beans (recipe on page 83) or with country-style ribs (recipe on page 85).

Makes about 2 cups

1½ cups sliced fresh or frozen rhubarb

1 cup blueberries

1½ tablespoons olive oil

½ large onion, finely chopped

½ cup dark brown sugar

4 ounces tomato sauce

¼ cup red wine vinegar or apple cider vinegar

¼ cup whiskey (optional)

⅛ cup soy sauce

⅛ cup honey

1 tablespoon Worcestershire sauce

1 teaspoon garlic powder

¼ teaspoon cayenne

½ teaspoon black pepper

In a saucepan, combine the rhubarb and blueberries, adding enough water to cover. Bring to a boil and cook uncovered until the rhubarb is soft, about 8 minutes. Using a potato masher or a fork, mash the mixture. Set aside.

Heat a large frying pan on medium-high heat. Add the olive oil and onions and fry until tender, about 4–6 minutes. Add the dark brown sugar, tomato sauce, vinegar, whiskey (if using), soy sauce, honey, Worcestershire sauce, garlic, cayenne, and black pepper. Mix well. Add the rhubarb-blueberry mixture. Turn the heat to low and cook for 10 minutes, removing the lid to thicken the sauce, if needed.

Rhubarb Simple Syrup

Simple syrup made with rhubarb is handy to add to drinks and in savory dishes. The rhubarb adds complexity to an otherwise plainly sweet addition to recipes.

Makes about 1 cup

½ cup water
1 cup sliced fresh or frozen rhubarb
½ cup granulated sugar

Mix the water, sliced rhubarb, and sugar in a small saucepan and bring to a boil. Reduce heat and simmer 12–15 minutes until the mixture has thickened. Strain through a fine sieve into a glass jar, pressing the rhubarb pulp to extract as much liquid as possible. Discard the solids or use in chutney or jam. Cool to room temperature and refrigerate. The syrup can be stored in the refrigerator for 2–3 weeks.

Rhubarb Mint Simple Syrup

Makes about 1½ cups

2 ¼ cups sliced fresh or frozen rhubarb
⅔ cup granulated sugar
Juice of 1 lemon and 1 tablespoon lemon zest
⅓ cup fresh mint leaves
¾ cup water

Add rhubarb to small saucepan with granulated sugar, lemon juice, lemon zest, mint leaves, and water. Simmer for 10 minutes until the rhubarb is soft. Take the pan off the burner and cool for 3–4 minutes. Pour mixture through a sieve and cool the liquid syrup in the refrigerator for 2 hours or more.

Strawberry Rhubarb Simple Syrup

Makes about 2 cups

1½ cups coarsely chopped fresh or frozen rhubarb
1½ cups hulled and diced strawberries
1 cup granulated sugar
1 cup water

Combine the rhubarb, strawberries, granulated sugar, and water in a saucepan. Bring to a hard simmer and continue for 10 minutes. Mash rhubarb with a fork or potato masher and strain the liquid mixture through a metal sieve to make a delightfully pink simple syrup. Cool before using. Store in a refrigerator.

Rhubarb Strawberry Syrup/Dessert Sauce

Cooks of yore knew a thing or two about flavor combinations. Strawberry and rhubarb make a classic and perennial favorite. Even if you prefer maple syrup on your pancakes, you might be swayed with this on your table. It's a jammy syrup that's tasty on pancakes and waffles or as a topping on pound cake, ice cream, and other desserts.

Makes about 3 cups

3 cups ½-inch slices fresh or frozen rhubarb
1 cup granulated sugar
⅓ cup water
1 cup sliced strawberries
1 tablespoon cornstarch dissolved in 2 tablespoons water
1 teaspoon vanilla

In a saucepan, bring rhubarb, strawberries, sugar, and water to a boil over medium-high heat. Reduce heat and cover, simmering for 10 minutes, stirring often. Add dissolved cornstarch. Cook and stir until mixture boils and thickens. Sauce will be slightly lumpy. Remove from heat, stir in vanilla. Spoon into clean glass jar and cover. Chill.

Rhubarb Blueberry Syrup/Dessert Sauce

Here's another addictive option for your breakfast pancakes or waffles and desserts, with the enticing, soothing taste of blueberries.

Makes about 3½ cups

3 cups ½-inch pieces fresh or frozen rhubarb
2 cups granulated sugar
8 ounces fresh blueberries

In medium-sized saucepan over medium-high heat, bring rhubarb and sugar to a boil for 10 minutes, stirring often. Stir in blueberries and return to a boil and continue until the blueberries lose their shape. Remove from heat and spoon into glass jars. This keeps in the refrigerator for up to a week. Alternatively, store in plastic food containers for freezing.

Kitchen Tips

FRESH OR FROZEN?

Using fresh, robust rhubarb is a great first step to tasty recipes. If your rhubarb season is short, you might also consider freezing rhubarb for later use (rhubarb preparation for freezing is on page 19). Using frozen rhubarb in recipes is simple—measure while frozen, thaw in a colander but do not press, and follow the usual recipe steps.

OVERCOOKED JAM

If your jam turns out hard and tacky, it was cooked over too hot a burner or for too long. Spoon the overcooked jam into a large saucepan. Add 1 cup of water and bring the mixture to a boil over medium heat, stirring to incorporate all of the water. Cook until the gelling point has been reached (217°F to 221°F, depending on how fluid you like it). Spoon into clean jars and process in a water bath if you are canning.

JAR PREPARATION

When you make a recipe, be sure to have jars ready to store your creations. To clean and prepare your jars, wash the empty jars in hot water with detergent and rinse well, or wash and dry them in a dishwasher. Make sure there is no unrinsed detergent residue left on the glass. This may cause unnatural flavors and colors.

All jams, jellies, and pickled products processed less than 10 minutes should be filled into sterile empty jars, according to the USDA. To sterilize empty jars after washing and rinsing them thoroughly, submerge them, right side up, in a boiling-water canner with the rack in the bottom. If you do not have a canner, use a wide, deep pot and place a wire rack of any type at the bottom to reduce the chance of breakage. Fill the canner or pot with enough warm water so it is 1 inch above the tops of the jars. Bring the water to a boil, and boil 10 minutes at altitudes of less than 1,000 feet. At higher elevations, boil 1 additional minute for each additional 1,000 feet of elevation. Reduce the heat under the canner and keep the jars in the hot water until it is time to fill them. Remove and drain hot sterilized jars one at a time, saving the hot water in the canner for processing filled jars if you are canning. Fill the sterilized jars with food, add lids, and tighten screw bands.

According to the USDA's "Principles of Home Canning," jars should be kept hot until ready to fill with food. Submerge the clean, empty jars in enough water to cover them in a large stockpot or boiling water canner. Bring the water to a simmer (180°F) and keep the jars in the simmering water until it is time to fill them with food. Alternatively, a dishwasher may be used for preheating jars if they are washed and dried on a complete regular cycle. Keep the jars in the closed dishwasher until needed for filling.

If you see a white film on the exterior surface of your jars it is likely caused by hard water mineral deposits. This film is easily removed by soaking jars several hours in a solution containing 1 cup of vinegar (5 percent acidity) per gallon of water prior to washing and preheating the jars.

PRESERVING AND CANNING

If you are new to canning, I highly recommend choosing a trustworthy canning resource when preserving foods such as the USDA's *Complete Guide to Home Canning*, available online (see references list). Most of the recipes for jams, chutneys, and preserves in this book are good candidates for canning preservation.

SPOON OR SHEET TEST

In these recipes, you will often need to check for your jam's readiness. To determine if your jam has reached its gelling point, in recipes made without added pectin, the sheet test, also known as the spoon test, is one method. Here's how it works: dip a cool metal spoon into the boiling jelly or jam mixture. Raise the spoon out of the steam, or about 12 inches above the pan. Turn the spoon so the liquid runs off the side. The jelly is done when the syrup forms 2 drops that flow together and sheet or hang off the edge of the spoon. Remove from heat.

TEMPERATURE TEST

Another method for readiness of jams is a temperature test. Use a jelly or candy thermometer and boil until mixture reaches the following temperatures at altitudes of:

Sea Level: 220°F

1,000 ft.: 218°F

2,000 ft.: 216°F

3,000 ft.: 214°F

4,000 ft.: 212°F

5,000 ft.: 211°F

6,000 ft.: 209°F

7,000 ft.: 207°F

8,000 ft.: 205°F

MEASUREMENTS

All recipe measurements in this book are in the imperial measurement system, which is standard in the US.

LIQUIDS

1 gallon = 4 quarts, 8 pints, 16 cups, 128 fl. oz., or 3.8 liters
1 quart = 2 pints, 4 cups, 32 fl. oz., 946 mL
1 pint = 2 cups, 16 fl. oz., 473 mL

POUNDS, OUNCES, GRAMS

1 pound = 16 oz., 455 gr.
¾ pound = 12 oz., 340 gr.

CUPS, TABLESPOONS, TEASPOONS, MILLILITERS

1 cup = 16 Tbsp., 48 tsp., 240 mL
¾ cup = 12 Tbsp., 36 tsp., 180 mL
⅔ cup = 10 ⅔ Tbsp., 32 tsp., 160 mL
½ cup = 8 Tbsp., 24 tsp., 120 mL
⅓ cup = 5 ⅓ Tbsp., 16 tsp., 80 mL
¼ cup = 4 Tbsp., 12 tsp., 60 mL
⅛ cup = 2 Tbsp., 6 tsp., 30 mL
1/16 cup = 1 Tbsp., 3 tsp., 15 mL

TEMPERATURE CONVERSION, FAHRENHEIT TO CELSIUS

500°F = 260°C

475°F = 246°C

450°F = 232°C

425°F = 218°C

400°F = 204°C

375°F = 190°C

350°F = 177°C

325°F = 163°C

300°F = 149°C

275°F = 135°C

250°F = 121°C

Acknowledgements

My deep appreciation goes the eaters out there who like rhubarb and created the demand for this book. I am now a forever fan of this refreshing taste of spring. Thank you to Laura McHugh and Lynn Rossy for helping test recipes; to Marty Townsend and Clark Swisher for diligently taste-testing every rhubarb creation I brought over; and for my husband, Terry Furstenau, for the same almost-daily contemplative work while I was writing this book. Thank you to Scherrie Goettsch for the archival rhubarb materials that helped so much. My gratitude goes to those who made publishing this book happen—especially Danielle Chiotti of Upstart Crow Literary and Anne Trubek of Belt Publishing.

Acknowledgements

References

In addition to the fine cooks in my family, dear friends who have consulted with me on recipes, and online sources, I am indebted to the following in creating this book. I especially appreciated the detailed horticultural information from Susan Mahr at the University of Wisconsin–Madison, and the history and uses of rhubarb from Clifford M. Foust's *Rhubarb: The Wondrous Drug*.

Arnarson, Alti. "Rhubarb: Is it Good for You? All You Need to Know." Healthline. 2024. https://www.healthline.com/nutrition/rhubarb#what-it-is.

Foust, Clifford M. *Rhubarb: The Wondrous Drug*. Vol. 191. Princeton University Press, 2014.

Hamilton, D.A. "A Little Paper on Rhubarb." University of Illinois Extension. https://www.ndsu.edu/pubweb/chiwonlee/plsc211/student%20papers/articles02/dhamilton/dhamilton.html.

H., David. "Did John Bartram Introduce Rhubarb to North America?" The Philadelphia Historic Plants Consortium. 2012. https://growinghistory.wordpress.com/2012/07/20/did-john-bartram-introduce-rhubarb-to-north-america/.

How to Grow Rhubarb from Seed. The Seed Collection. 2021. https://www.theseedcollection.com.au/blog/how-to-grow-rhubarb-from-seed.

Kelley, Laura. "Rhubarb's Silk Road History." *Silk Road Gourmet*. 2014. https://www.silkroadgourmet.com/rhubarb/.

Lo, Vivienne, and Penelope Barrett. "Cooking Up Fine Remedies: On the Culinary Aesthetic in a Sixteenth-century Chinese Materia Medica." *Medical History* 49, no. 4 (2005): 395–422.

Mahr, Susan. "Rhubarb, *Rheum rhabarbarum.*" University of Wisconsin-Madison Horticulture. https://hort.extension.wisc.edu/articles/rhubarb-rheum-rhabarbarum/.

Nir, Sarah Maslin. "How Rhubarb Conquered Germany, Then the World." *New York Times*, June 1, 2024. https://www.nytimes.com/2024/06/01/world/europe/germany-rhubarb-rap.html.

Rundell, Maria Eliza Ketelby. *A New System of Domestic Cookery: formed upon principles of economy and adapted to the use of private families*. J. Murray, 1824. Google Books.

USDA Complete Guide to Home Canning. National Center for Home Preservation, University of Georgia. 2015. https://nchfp.uga.edu/resources/category/usda-guide.

About the Author

Nina Mukerjee Furstenau is a food journalist and writer with interest in food, identity, and culture. She has written five books, including her memoir, *Biting Through the Skin: An Indian Kitchen in America's Heartland*, which won the MFK Fisher Book Award, among other accolades. In addition to the books *Green Chili & Other Impostors*, *Food & Culture*, *Tasty! Mozambique*, and *Savor Missouri*, her podcast, *Canned Peaches*, is available through NPR. She also writes stories and essays for magazines and current media. You can find her work at ninafurstenau.com.

Belt Publishing

beltpublishing.com